Too Greedy for Adam Smith

*CEO Pay and the
Demise of Capitalism*

Steven Bavaria

Hungry Hollow Books
Chestnut Ridge, New York

Too Greedy for Adam Smith
Copyright © 2015 by Steven Bavaria

ISBN-13: 978-0692491256
ISBN-10: 0692491252

Cover design and graphics by Mark Cavanagh

Hungry Hollow Books
Chestnut Ridge, NY 10952

Table of Contents

4

PREFACE

EMPEROR'S NEW CLOTHES, AND OTHER ISSUES

This is a book I have been expecting to **read**, rather than **write**, for many years. As the chapter title above suggests, I view this as an "Emperor's New Clothes" sort of story. The main message of the book – *that the way CEO pay gets set is totally inconsistent with how other wages and prices get determined throughout our free market economy* – seems so obvious that it hardly needs to be pointed out.

But just as the obvious is ignored in the Hans Christian Andersen fairy tale, what seems apparent to me and to many others – that CEOs are paid far more than is actually or economically required to induce capable people to fill their jobs – never seems to be recognized as a serious issue that hurts our economy in many ways and needs to be addressed at a national level.

Less obvious but equally important is the political danger this represents to our capitalistic, free market system going forward. When our corporate ruling elite sends out a continuous and consistent message that the normal economic rules that apply to everyone else do not apply to them, it is a clear invitation to the rest of us to change our system so we all can enjoy the same generous "safety net" that they enjoy.

Some excellent "serious" writers, like Michael Dorff of Southwestern Law School, and Lucian Bebchuk and Jesse Fried of Harvard and University of California, Berkeley Law Schools, respectively, have written valuable books about how the excessive compensation paid to CEOs over many decades has been unwarranted in terms of the shareholder value received, and how the so-called "pay for performance" movement has essentially failed.

Unfortunately, I believe the topic of uncontrolled executive pay and its negative impact on our economy and our society is too serious to be left to the "serious" writers. So this is intended to be a simple book that explains to ordinary readers, in plain English, how CEO pay gets determined, and more important, how totally inconsistent that process is with the way in which our free enterprise system sets other prices, including everyone else's wages.

I have tried to describe simply and clearly a rather sad yet amazing irony: ***The most capitalistic country in the world determines the pay for its corporate leaders in a manner fundamentally inconsistent with the normal rules of capitalism (law of supply and demand, etc.).***

I will show how conflict-of-interest-ridden "sweetheart" deals are treated as unethical and illegal in most business situations, and yet are the norm in corporate boardrooms and compensation committees in setting CEO pay. Corporations that would fire their purchasing manager in a heartbeat if he (or she) rented office space from a cousin or crony for twice the market rate think nothing of having directors who are themselves conflicted sit on compensation committees and award pay packages to their CEOs that are a multiple of what normal labor market economics would require to fill the job.

To explain this we will introduce some basic economic concepts, like the requirement that to be a genuine "arms-length" transaction in a free enterprise system you need to have people on both sides of the bargaining table actively attempting to get the "best deal" for their side. This requirement is routinely met in most of the transactions we all engage in throughout our lives (including negotiating our own pay). But this key element of the bargaining process is routinely missing in the setting of CEO pay, where nobody actively and objectively represents the company and its shareholders, because of inherent conflicts of interest and "group think" tendencies firmly entrenched in the corporate governance process.

We will also discuss how dangerous all this is for our economy and our society. The downside is not that we just have too many rich people who haven't earned it. Far worse is the incentive that these "mega payouts" give to CEOs and their top officers to "swing for the fences" and do big deals that often serve little economic purpose except to generate huge bonuses, stock options and "golden parachutes" for executives and their

Wall Street enablers. The social overhead costs of the transactions (layoffs, factory closings, former "company towns" now without a company) which in an earlier era would have been important considerations to more modestly paid CEOs with a longer-term focus, are now left out of the equation.

Finally, we discuss the socio-political dangers of our fellow citizens coming to realize that the economic ruling elite has a different set of rules applying to them than the ones that apply to everyone else. As voters see that people at the top of the corporate pyramid live and work in a world with lots of upside potential but little or no downside risk, they will want that for themselves.

That's why these issues should concern Republicans and conservatives as much as they do Democrats and liberals. If we want our nation to continue to embrace free enterprise principles, and to reject so-called "socialist" or redistributionist policies, then we have to be rigorous in ensuring that corporate leaders, who should be shining examples of capitalist values, actually practice what they preach with regard to their own compensation.

My goal in writing this, and especially in doing so in a somewhat breezy, simplified style, is to move the topic beyond the two groups that currently are most aware of the issues :

- CEOs and boards of directors themselves, who are not inclined to do anything about it other than to ignore or defend current practices, and
- Legal, business and academic researchers and writers, whose books and articles may be over the heads of ordinary readers, and therefore don't really impact the public and political arena as much as they should.

Hence my interest in popularizing this issue so ordinary people who are not experts in economics, corporate law or governance can still grasp the concepts, express their views and engage in dialogue about it.[1] With

---

[1] I realize there is a wide range of understanding about these issues and the economic principles that underlie them. For those who "get it" immediately, are able to see the emperor's skimpy wardrobe and don't need the economics lessons or my detailed connecting of the dots, I have included a "Condensed

the gap between the very wealthy and everyone else continuing to grow, and runaway CEO pay helping to accelerate it, we need to move this topic beyond the boardrooms, business schools and law schools, and into broader public discussion.

It is hard to fix something unless you first label and describe it correctly. Paying CEOs far more than is economically required is a misuse of corporate assets and a serious breach of the fiduciary duty of directors to safeguard shareholder interests. As investors and citizens, we should appreciate it and address it as such.

Version" as an appendix that summarizes the whole book. Feel free to skip directly to it.

INTRODUCTION

HOW EXECUTIVE PAY IS
DESTROYING FREE ENTERPRISE

This book is about how out-of-control executive pay is destroying free enterprise in America.

It is not an attack on capitalism.[2] Nor am I suggesting that getting rich is inconsistent with a healthy free enterprise economy. In fact, capitalism is the only economic system that is consistent with a democratic political system, and that allows people from all sorts of backgrounds the opportunity to maximize their own personal economic potential.

But how people accumulate great wealth is very important, for a number of reasons. Think of the economy as a huge game, like

---

[2] The terms "capitalism" and "free enterprise" are used interchangeably throughout the book.

baseball or football. Getting rich is the equivalent of scoring a touchdown or hitting a home run. Getting really rich is like hitting a grand slam. In a game, the home run or the touchdown only counts if you score it legally, according to the rules. If your team is off side or commits interference downfield, your touchdown doesn't count. If your hit is outside the foul lines, or hit with a bat that you "corked" or otherwise tampered with, again the runs don't score and the play is disallowed.

This is basic to the idea of any game, and is the fundamental difference between an organized game, sport or other contest (bridge, chess, etc.) and mere chaos. People may run around a field, do whatever they want and it may be fun, entertaining, diverting, or whatever. But without agreed-upon rules and structure, and umpires or referees to enforce them, it is not a game or sport.

The rules and structure of a game are critical if we expect anyone to take the results of the game seriously. That is especially true if it is a game where there is money or something else of value at stake depending on the game's outcome. Consider the millions of dollars wagered – legally and illegally – on the Super Bowl or the World Series each year. Would those bets be placed if the fans making those wagers had doubts about whether the game was fair and the rules would be applied? Would fans spend millions of dollars and countless hours watching and following sports if they didn't trust the outcome was arrived at fairly? If the idea ever took hold that a major sport or game wasn't being played fairly and according to its rules, it would quickly lose its following and its multi-billion dollar revenue stream would dry up.

One particular game that demands public faith in its fairness is a lottery. People who buy lottery tickets know that there is only one chance in a million (or more) that they will win a mega-prize. But if they ever thought the game was fixed, and their odds were zero in a million rather than one in a million, the game would be over and they'd all stop playing.

The economy is also a game, admittedly a very serious one, where people play for high stakes: their livelihoods, their futures and those of their children, their homes, their life savings, their retirements. Even more than any major sport, our economy has to maintain its credibility with ordinary people if they are to continue to play the game. "Playing the game" in a representative democracy like ours means more than just showing up for work and participating in the economy. It also requires voters to continue to support laws that maintain a competitive, capitalistic system.

If people begin to feel the game is rigged, that everyone in the system no longer has a chance of winning the economic lottery for themselves, or that the rules are not being applied fairly across the board, then free enterprise will lose its popular support.

That is the danger America faces now, as more and more Americans come to believe that a different set of rules applies to the very rich than applies to everyone else.

Unfortunately, people who feel that way are correct, although they may not know why they are correct, or exactly which rules don't apply to the people at the top of the economic pyramid, even though they apply to everybody else.

This book will explain what the basic rules of our economic system are, and most importantly, how many of them ***are not*** *allowed to operate* in the boardrooms across America when it comes to setting compensation for our corporate elite.

We will also discuss how this is hurting us and our country politically, socially and economically, and how dangerous it is to our future. We will discuss how paying people too much results in bad economic decisions. (We don't mean "too much" from an ethical or moral standpoint, but "too much" compared to what the free enterprise system would actually pay CEOs if the free enterprise system were allowed to operate freely in the executive compensation arena.)

In other words, motivation matters. Giving executives incentives where a single deal can reap them tens or hundreds of millions of dollars in excess pay often encourages them to make decisions that are good for themselves personally but not necessarily so for the company. It can promote a "swing for the fences" mentality where the prospect of a huge short-term payout for the CEO may lead to taking risks that are inconsistent with the long-term well-being and security of the company and its constituent community (customers, employees, shareholders.)

But excess pay does not just provide perverse incentives that cause CEOs to make bad decisions. It also undermines the confidence that ordinary people have in our free market system. If people feel the normal rules of supply and demand, including what classical economists called "the iron law of wages," operate at their own personal level, while a different set of rules operates for the people at the top, that erodes their belief in capitalism.

Many people have learned first-hand how classical economics works. They have been fired or had their jobs eliminated because their business contracted or was merged or bought out, or moved to another part of the world. If they were fortunate they got severance or "outplacement," perhaps for the equivalent of a few weeks or months pay, even if their performance was outstanding. So they know how free market capitalism works.

But then these same people observe that when the CEOs of major companies are removed for incompetence or their companies fail, instead of getting a few weeks or months of severance, they typically receive millions or tens of millions of dollars in "golden parachutes" and other sweetheart deals.

You don't have to be an economist to know that what goes on in the boardrooms is more like what we often call "socialism" than it is "capitalism." If capitalism incorporates the idea of "risk and reward," that you only get the potential rewards of success if you also bear the risk of failure, then it is clear to most people that one of the few places in the business world where that does NOT happen is in our corporate boardrooms.

Corporate CEOs, whose pay is set by boards made up of other corporate CEOs, are privileged in that they have enormous upside in terms of "reward" but very little if any downside risk. When was the last time anyone ever heard of a board firing a chief executive without providing them a lucrative exit deal on the way out?

The danger in this is more than just having too many previously incompetent but extremely rich former CEOs crowding the locker rooms and pro shops of exclusive country clubs. The real danger is that ordinary Americans, jaded by how the corporate ruling class has jettisoned the "risk" in the risk/reward concept for themselves in their executive suites, may decide to discard it for everyone throughout our political and economic system.

And why shouldn't they? If voters conclude that CEOs and other top-of-the-pyramid executives have essentially conspired with each other to ensure a system where (1) they get paid more money than they would if normal economic forces were allowed to operate and (2) that they get it whether they perform or not, then wouldn't we expect those voters to say "Hey, I want that too?"

Can anyone blame ordinary people for listening to or supporting politicians who want to replace traditional free enterprise-oriented policies with what conservative commentators might label "cradle-to-grave" or "redistributionist" social policies if they see that the ruling elite has essentially done that for itself?

That's why the issues raised here are just as critical to traditional Republicans as they are to Democrats. Radio talk show hosts and other commentators complain at times that our capitalistic system is under attack. They are right. But the really serious attack is from the forces at the top, not the bottom, who by rigging the rules of the game to benefit themselves, risk undermining faith in the integrity of the game for everyone.

It is not a criticism of capitalism to insist that economic participants play fairly and abide by the rules, any more than it is a criticism of baseball, football, bicycling or any other sport to try to eliminate cheaters who use steroids or other illegal performance enhancing substances, or coaches who try to pay off umpires or referees.

The author has been a banker, writer, financial executive and active investor for over forty years. He has benefitted from and indeed reveres free enterprise, especially having lived, worked and travelled throughout the world and seen the results in countries that had too little of it.

So this book, while it contains harsh criticism of the way boardroom pay and compensation practices have evolved, is in no way an attack on capitalism and free enterprise. Rather it is an argument for expanding it: to let free enterprise play the same role in setting the price level of CEO compensation that it plays in setting other prices throughout the economy.

CHAPTER 1

ECONOMICS 001:
HOW THINGS ARE SUPPOSED
TO WORK

For those who have studied economics and actually taken "Economics 101" and other courses, this chapter may seem rudimentary. Feel free to skip it.

I'm calling this "Economics 001" just to highlight how basic it is. But basic is OK, since economics is actually pretty simple. It is based on a few fundamental principles of human behavior, which are assumed to be true in most instances:

- Buyers, in general, prefer to pay *the lowest price* they can for an item.
- Sellers, on the other hand, prefer to charge *the highest price* they can.

But actual prices for most items end up getting set somewhere in the middle:

- *Low enough* that buyers will be willing and able to pay for them, yet
- *High enough* that sellers will be willing to make the item available

So every price at which a good or service is sold throughout our economy represents a *compromise* between buyers and sellers. Not as low as the price buyers would prefer, nor as high as the price sellers would prefer. But a price somewhere in the middle high enough to induce sellers to make the product available for sale, and low enough to induce buyers to pay for it. An economist would say the price "clears the market" (i.e. allows transactions to freely take place at that price).

Besides this universal human instinct to "buy low" and "sell high," there are several other basic economic principles that logically and intuitively flow from these first two. Taken together they explain how markets manage to compromise the "buy low/sell high" instincts of buyers and sellers and achieve market-clearing prices, so that products get sold and business takes place.

The most important principles are the ones enshrined in the expression "the law of supply and demand." What the so-called "law" of supply and demand refers to is the dynamic impact that changes in price have on both the demand for goods and services by buyers, and the supply of goods and services by sellers. This law, or principle, describes what is – once again – pretty much common sense:

- When the *price of an item goes up*, that tends to discourage buyers and they end up buying less. This occurs for a variety of reasons: some can't afford it or can't afford as much of it; others may find that at the higher price it makes sense to substitute other, cheaper items for it. Economists would call that a decrease in "demand" for the product.

- Meanwhile, the higher price has the opposite effect on sellers, who will want to sell more of it because the higher price means greater profits for them. It may also induce additional sellers who did not previously sell that item to begin doing so. Economists call this an increase in the "supply" of the product.

- But when the *price goes down* it has the opposite effect. Buyers can afford more of it at the lower price, and may even look for ways to substitute it for higher priced alternatives. Economists call this an increase in demand for the product.

- Meanwhile sellers, seeing the price drop, will want to sell less of it. The more marginal suppliers, who are less efficient and make less of a profit margin on their sales, will generally be the first to drop out of the market. While the reduction may not be uniform across the board, in the aggregate the price drop will lead to a *decrease* in the supply of the item.

So far we have been looking at what happens to the supply of an item (i.e. sellers' propensity to sell it) and the demand for it (i.e. buyers' propensity to buy it) if its price changes. But that's only looking at it from one direction. We can also turn the analysis around and examine what happens to the price if the supply or demand changes.

For example, suppose a town that had only one car dealership all of a sudden has a second one open up. With two dealers trying to sell cars, we would expect the increased competition to bring the price of cars down. Expressing this as another economic principle, we would say that increasing the supply of an item usually leads to a decrease in its price.

Now consider the situation where a town with two car dealerships has one close down, leaving it with only one. Fewer dealerships means a *decreased supply* of cars in town, due to less competition among sellers, and car buyers will not be able to negotiate as good a price as they could have when there were two dealers. So car prices will likely increase. To generalize, a drop in supply of an item leads to its price increasing.

Demand can also go up and down, with its own effect on prices. Suppose in this town there is a factory that closes down, putting people out of work and causing some families to seek greener pastures by moving elsewhere. Fewer families in town means a reduction in the demand for cars. But with the same number of car dealers as before and fewer potential buyers, car prices are likely to drop as car dealers now have to compete harder to satisfy the smaller demand.

On the other hand, if instead of closing, the local factory expands, and instead of an exodus from town you have more people arriving to seek the newly available jobs, that will *increase the demand* for cars (and for homes, groceries and everything else for that matter). So – other things being equal[3] – the price of cars will likely go up because now there will be more competition among buyers to purchase them.

The prices of those other goods – houses, groceries, haircuts – will all probably go up too, with the influx of new people in town competing to buy them. But the price increase may only be temporary if the *increased demand* for all those items causes new grocery stores and barber shops to open up, or induces contractors to build more new homes to supply the increased demand for housing.

If you are a thoughtful person, you may be saying to yourself: "Well, all those little rules seem to make sense, but what happens in a real economy? Don't some of the rules actually work at cross-purposes to each other? Or cancel each other out?"

---

[3] "Other things being equal" is an important phrase in economics that means "assuming other factors don't change." If you want to really impress your colleagues, you can express the phrase in Latin: "Ceteris paribus."

Bingo! Yes, that is in fact exactly what happens. All these rules sort of run together, sometimes multiple rules applying to the same transaction, so that the result is usually a series of compromises between buyers and sellers. Economists describe this as reaching "equilibrium," the point where prices are just able to match up the requirements of both buyers and sellers and the "deal gets done," whatever the "deal" is: buying a car or a home, selling groceries, getting a haircut, etc.

Returning to our examples up above, we saw how having a second car dealer open up in town would have the effect of lowering car prices, due to increased competition and more people trying to sell cars to the same population. We didn't ask the question of why the second car dealer moved to town. Most likely, the new dealer opened its business because the previously prevailing level of prices (i.e. back when it was a "one-dealer" town) was so high. So we see two rules working together here in this simple example: (1) high prices leading to an increase in supply, and (2) the increase in supply leading to lower prices. Where they finally settle is the "equilibrium" point, where prices are high enough for both dealers to make a fair profit and stay in business, but low enough to induce local townspeople to buy at least the minimal number of cars each year to support the two businesses.

But it doesn't stop there. The lower prices may eventually cause additional buyers who may not have been able to consider owning a car when prices were higher to change their minds and start shopping for cars; maybe people who previously never had a car, or people with older cars who now see the potential trade-in cost more reasonable, or families with one car who will now be able to afford a second one.

So now we've seen (1) high prices leading to increased supply, (2) increased supply leading to lower prices, (3) the lower prices leading to an increased demand, and (4) the increased demand leading to higher prices again. This will lead to a further increase in supply and the cycle may continue all over again, especially if the economy keeps growing. In our example, the increased demand for cars eventually pushes automobile prices back up again. The growing demand and resulting higher prices may attract a third car dealer into town, which in turn will start to bring prices back down. And of course the new car dealer may employ a few townspeople, giving them additional money to spend, which they end up spending to buy cars, helping to push car prices back up closer to where they were before.

As noted above, it is all about achieving equilibrium: prices not so high that nobody can afford cars, but not so low that dealers can't afford to stay in business. Changes in any of these factors: price levels, the supply of cars, and the demand for cars, can be catalysts for changes in the others. All the "micro" decisions by individual buyers (what to buy, how much to buy, what to pay) and by individual sellers (what to sell, how much to sell, how to price it) end up creating millions of little equilibrium points (i.e. "prices") where transactions take place throughout the economy.

Prices are constantly being adjusted for all kinds of reasons, but usually in response to an action or occurrence that reflects one of the simple basic principles we listed above. It is the inter-action of these basic principles that explains most of what goes on in a free enterprise economy.

In some ways economics is a bit like the geometry you studied in high school. Remember how in geometry there were a few simple basic assumptions, called "postulates," that you could use, over and over again, along with deductive logic, to construct proofs of how everything else in the geometric world worked? Economics is similar, in that these basic assumptions about human behavior can be used to construct models for how economic markets work, and how prices of goods and services are set in a capitalistic system (aka "free enterprise.")

These basic themes, buyers' desire to buy more and more the lower prices go, and sellers' willingness to sell more and more the higher prices go, and vice versa when prices move the opposite way, are repeated over and over every single day in our economy.

We have mentioned that economists call these principles – how price movements affect sale and purchase decisions, and vice versa – the "law of supply and demand." Adam Smith, who is often referred to as the "father of modern economics," identified these principles in his epic work *The Wealth of Nations* in 1776. He described the effect of all these micro decisions in creating optimal results for the economy at large as the "invisible hand."

What is remarkable about how free markets work (regardless of whether it's called "supply and demand" or the "invisible hand") is that you start out with everyone making choices based on what's best for themselves personally[4] – the lowest price if you're a buyer, the highest price if you're a seller – and through the workings of the market you end up with prices that work and an economy that functions.

At least it does most of the time. Sometimes political and economic commentators forget that supply and demand and the other features of our free market system don't work automatically all by themselves any more than a bunch of kids on a field will automatically start

---

[4] This "what's best for themselves personally" is a big deal, as we will see later. Free enterprise, supply and demand and the "invisible hand" only work if there are *two parties to every transaction* trying to get the best deal that they can for themselves.

playing baseball or football if there aren't any agreed-upon rules and a referee or umpire to enforce them. In later chapters, we will discuss these underlying rules and, especially, what happens when they are ignored or there is nobody to enforce them.

But before that, in the next chapter we will discuss how supply and demand works – or, at least, is supposed to work – in the labor market.

CHAPTER 2

LABOR COSTS AND THE "INVISIBLE HAND"

We all think of ourselves as very special, and few things are as important to us as our own jobs and, especially, what we get paid. But from the standpoint of economists and the economy, we – more specifically, our "labor" – are just another item to be bought and sold in the marketplace. In other words, the demand for our services and what people will pay us to work for them depends on the law of supply and demand just like any other product and service in the marketplace.

Indeed, because our job prospects and potential wage levels are so personal and important to each of us, most people are probably more aware of the economic forces affecting their own career and pay prospects than they are of the workings of other parts of the economy.

So what we are saying here will not come as a surprise to most readers. The basic theme of this book is simple. All those economic principles we discussed in the last chapter about how prices get determined in a free market economy (supply and demand, the "invisible hand," etc.) also apply to how wages and salaries are determined. At least they should. But there is one glaring exception: the setting of the CEO's pay in major corporations.

But before we can discuss how the setting of CEO pay *violates* traditional economic principles, first we must explain how the setting of virtually everyone else's pay *does conform* to normal economic principles. Fortunately, this is easy because most people already know it from their own experience (some of it painful, like during the recent Great Recession).

If we called the last chapter "Economics 001," then we can call this chapter "Labor Economics 001." None of it is rocket science.

Let's start with the basic economic principles we outlined in the last chapter: (1) most people would prefer to pay as little as possible for whatever they buy, and (2) most sellers would like to charge as much as possible for whatever they are selling. That applies to **wages** as well. Most workers would like to get paid as much as they can for the work they do (i.e. for *selling* their labor). Meanwhile, most employers (i.e. the *buyers* of that labor) would prefer to pay as little as possible to attract the employees they need to run their businesses.

Many of the applications of supply and demand principles that we discussed in "Economics 001" apply directly to the labor markets. For example, if there is a shortage of a certain type of skill in a local labor market, then the pay rate (i.e. the price) for that type of specialty will tend to go up, as businesses compete with one another to hire the people with the skill that is in short supply. Other workers, observing this, may take steps to acquire the skill by enrolling in training courses, or those living further away who already have that expertise may decide to commute further or even move to the area in order to take the available jobs. As that happens and more skilled workers become available, it will alleviate the scarcity that was driving up pay rates, and starting pay for that job should fall back down to its normal pre-shortage level.

This is the same supply/demand cycle we saw in the last chapter: A shortage of something – in this case, skilled workers – causes the price (pay rate) to rise as buyers – in this case, employers – bid up the price for those workers. But the higher pay rate attracts additional people into the workforce, thus meeting the labor shortage and bringing wage rates back down to an equilibrium level. The "invisible hand" at work.

The opposite scenario occurs when there is a surplus of workers in general, or a surplus of workers with a particular skill or experience level. Having more workers available in a particular trade than there are actual jobs means there will be more applicants than are needed competing for each job. That will tend to depress wage rates, since employers know there will be plenty of applicants to choose from to fill any vacancies. Hence, there is no reason to raise the pay from whatever the current rate already is. This is the opposite situation from the one just described where a shortage of workers created competition among hiring companies for the available workers.

The overhang of excess workers competing for the available jobs can reduce or eliminate the bargaining leverage workers have to demand higher pay from employers, since both sides, employers and employees, know that anyone's potential replacement is waiting outside to fill the job if it becomes vacant.

In a global economy, "waiting outside" can mean 5,000 miles away, if the job can be outsourced abroad. But the effect on the employee's bargaining power is the same. This is why so many American workers (but not the CEOs) have seen their wages stagnate, even when the economy or their own employer's business has been growing.

In a traditional growing economy, some of these unemployed workers would look to move to new communities where there was a shortage of workers. With workers in shorter supply, not only would more jobs be available there, but wages would likely be above average as well. The new workers would arrive, take the surplus jobs, and help to re-balance the supply and demand of workers in that area. With the shortage of workers alleviated, wages would tend to return to a more normal level. Meanwhile, back home where they had previously lived, the exodus of unemployed workers would have removed the overhang of surplus labor from that market, increasing the bargaining position of the existing workers who were still there. That would have the effect of lifting wage rates in that community back to a more normal "equilibrium" level.

That's the theory. Large-scale migration, like we saw in the nineteenth century or after World War 2 involving the relocation of millions of people, is less widespread now as tighter entry restrictions have made it more difficult and dangerous to cross international borders. But people and businesses constantly move from one area of the country to another to seek better career and business opportunities. These "micro" movements, all individual decisions by workers, their families and the businesses that hire them, are guided by the same principles of supply and demand, the desire to pay as little as possible if you're a buyer (or employer), or charge (earn) as much as possible if you're a seller (employee), that we discussed earlier.

The role of Adam Smith's "invisible hand" may sometimes appear less obvious in the labor markets than in the market for more tangible products. That's because hiring people, as opposed to buying goods and services, involves a closer personal relationship between the buyer/employer and the seller/employee. Negotiating salaries, benefits and other employment terms is generally a private transaction, agreed upon confidentially between the hiring manager and the employee. Employers usually ask employees to keep the details of their compensation private, and professional and managerial level employees normally do. Possible exceptions might be public employees, whose pay is often a matter of public record, and members of unions working under contracts with pay rates that are uniform and widely known.

As a result, there can be a lot of variation in what a company pays it employees, from one worker to another. A group of people doing similar jobs at the same company may each have a different salary reflecting a range of factors, including:

- When they were hired. Was it at a time when the labor market was tight (i.e. fewer workers than job openings) and starting pay was higher as companies bid up the price to hire new workers, or was the labor market slack (more workers than available jobs)?

- Years of service with the company. One might expect experienced workers, who have been getting raises each year since they started their jobs, to make more than newly hired, less experienced workers. (But not always, especially in inflationary periods. See below.)
- Rate of inflation. During high inflation periods, companies often lag behind the inflation rate in raising the pay of their existing workers. But external hiring rates – what they have to pay new workers – are often immediately affected by inflation. So you can have the opposite effect to that described in the previous bullet point, where new workers "still wet behind the ears" end up being paid more than their experienced colleagues who started some years earlier but whose raises have not kept up with inflation. This was a big issue in the 1980s, but is less so now.
- Education and training, previous jobs and professional experience prior to being hired.

- The employer's perception that the employee is (or is not) at risk of being hired away by another employer. Some employees are more aggressive about asking for higher pay, using outside comparisons, and giving their employer the impression that they are "flight risks," while other employees are more content to sit back and accept whatever raises their employers give them. Which strategy works best often depends on the culture and attitude of the particular employer.

Although these factors may cause pay rates within a company (or a region or industry) to vary somewhat, even for the same job, there is still fundamental adherence to the basic economic principles of supply and demand. Most employers, despite pay inconsistencies between some workers and others, try to achieve the lowest labor cost they can.

"Lowest labor cost" in this context may have some caveats. It does not necessarily mean literally the lowest pay on a given day to attract anyone at all to do the job. Most modern employers (in developed countries, at least) do not operate Dickensian workhouses that pay the absolute lowest wages they can possibly get away with. Employers adopt various types of hiring strategies, depending on what industry they are in, the level of the positions being filled, how technically difficult the work is, the state of the local job market, and especially, how critical a particular position is to the overall success of the business.

For example, suppose a large part of Company A's business requires a dependable but fairly unskilled, easy-to-train workforce. Suppose the company also knows there is a healthy supply of willing, entry-level workers available in its local job market, so filling vacancies and training replacements is fairly straight-forward. Company A may conclude that the target range of pay for this job (i.e. the top and bottom of the range that will attract and keep employees in these positions) is between $40,000 and $45,000.

In this case, the company might be inclined to take a standardized approach to filling the job and offer every candidate a salary at the lower end of the scale, i.e. $40,000. Its reasoning might be that since the jobs are pretty undifferentiated and it is easy to attract and train new workers whenever they need them, then why would they need to stretch and pay more than the minimum required?

Meanwhile suppose Company B is in the same region and job market, but has a more complicated business and production process that requires workers with slightly more skill and training than Company A. Recruiting in the same basic job market, they may also conclude that the pay range to attract the applicants they want is $40,000-45,000. But for them, recruiting and retaining the more superior candidates within the hiring pool is critical to their business, so Company B may choose to be flexible about going above the minimum of $40,000 to be sure they get the candidates they really want.

Neither company's approach is necessarily better than the other. Company A realizes they merely need candidates who fulfill the basic job requirements, and as long as they can attract them successfully, there is no strategic reason to pay more than the minimum. Company B has concluded that their business success depends on recruiting superior candidates, so it is strategically necessary that their recruiters have flexibility to offer candidates whatever it takes (within the overall approved range) to hire the talented workers they need.

In both cases the companies are following the economic principle we outlined, of paying the "lowest price" they can in order to attract the employees they need to achieve their business strategy. We are not saying that free market economic principles dictate a company should pay the absolute lowest amount they can get away with to get any "warm body" into the job. Companies set the standards for what quality of employees they need, and then figure out what the labor market requires them to pay to attract that level of employee. If it is a uniquely high quality of employee, then the "lowest price" that the labor market dictates in that instance may still be a very high rate of pay, relative to the market as a whole.

Whatever that rate of pay dictated by the market turns out to be, a rational employer (i.e. the proverbial "rational consumer" that economists talk about) will pay it. But they will not willingly pay more than that. Deliberately paying more than you have to pay for something is an "irrational" act, from an economic perspective. Rational buyers do not pay more than "the market" requires them to, and rational sellers do not charge less than they can get, again determined by "the market." Where it gets tricky is determining what is "the market," or what is the "lowest price" the market is actually setting for the item you want to buy.

For example the "spot" price for the one-time delivery of an item may be X, while the price to have someone contract to provide you with a consistent, regular supply of that item for some future time period may be more than X. A company that agrees to pay the higher price in order to get a steady supply is still being a rational consumer, since they are paying the lowest price they can for what they need. In their case "what they need" is not just the item itself on a particular date, but a dependable supply of it over time. In other words, "lowest price" can be a slippery concept.

For example, let's take another look at Company A, whose basic work requirements were so simple they could confidently adopt a policy to offer all new employees the minimum of the range on a "take-it-or-leave-it" basis, knowing that approach would get them the workforce they needed.

Suppose elsewhere within Company A there is a department responsible for designing and engineering the firm's product and maintaining its competitive edge within its industry. The people working in that department hold the company's future in their hands, or maybe in their brains or imaginations. Company A will probably take a more aggressive approach to recruiting and paying these critical employees than it does to hiring the production line workers whose jobs it considers, in contrast, fairly rudimentary and easily filled.

Let's assume the salary range for recruiting these high-powered design engineers is $150,000 to $300,000. Where within that broad range Company A actually pays specific candidates will depend on a range of factors, as we saw earlier, including:

- Each one's education, background and experience,
- How competitive the market for design engineers is at the time they are hired,

- Whether the company perceives them as possible "flight risks" in terms of other firms trying to hire them away, and
- How aggressive some candidates are in negotiating their starting pay and subsequent raises.

Whether trying to hire one of these high-powered design engineers or one of the lower-paid production workers, the recruiter's job is the same. It is to try to find the "sweet spot," that salary figure which is high enough to attract the candidate and make them truly want to join the company and work diligently. Too low a figure and the candidate may turn down the job. Too high a figure, and the recruiter is (1) wasting the company's money paying more than is necessary to hire the desired candidate, and (2) creating potential organizational problems if the candidate's pay level becomes a precedent for other new hires or existing staff.

Obviously this is not much of an issue in the hiring of lower echelon staff, especially if there are clear-cut salary ranges for different jobs. In our examples, for instance, it doesn't hurt the company much if a recruiter ends up offering a candidate $43,000 when, if pushed, they might have been willing to take the job for only $41,000. Nobody expects the "invisible hand" to be able to set prices or wage rates that accurately. Nor will anyone within company management worry much about whether they are "wasting" the firm's money by paying someone $43,000 who might have been willing to do the job for $41,000.

The higher you go up the organizational ladder, of course, the more money is at stake, and the more attention is given to hiring decisions and pay packages. For Company A's design engineers, you can be sure that lots of analysis and discussion goes into deciding whether to offer a candidate $150,000, $200,000, or $250,000. Besides those factors mentioned above, the discussion would also include questions like:

- What's the candidate's salary history and how much are they currently paid?
- How much do we need to pay them to leave their job and join Company A?
- How much are other employees at Company A paid who already do similar jobs?

- Will it upset our internal wage structure if we pay the new candidate too much?
- What's the turnover rate for people doing this job at Company A?
- Are people leaving because we aren't paying enough?

Ideally, the goal is to find that "sweet spot" where you are offering a salary just high enough to motivate the candidate to come and work for your company, but no more than is necessary.

"Sweet spot" is just another way of saying equilibrium – that price point that clears the market and is not too high to scare away buyers, or too low to discourage sellers. And as we've seen, if we are talking about the labor markets, just substitute "employee" for sellers and "employer" for buyers.

In our next chapter we will talk about motivation, and how important it is that there be a "rational" buyer and seller on each side of the transaction. We will also see what happens when that is not the case: when the person on one side of the bargaining table negotiates hard to get a good deal, but the person on the other side of the table is not similarly motivated to get a good deal for their side.

CHAPTER 3

IT TAKES TWO TO TANGO

In all of the examples we have discussed so far, there have been two parties to the bargain, each with a different goal. A seller who wants to maximize what they are paid, and a buyer who wants to minimize what they have to pay. It is through that dynamic tension, multiplied millions of times per day, that prices and wages get set across the whole economy, and the economic system functions.

Free enterprise is based on the idea that **both sides to the transaction care about the outcome**, and each negotiates to achieve its own best result. In this chapter we will discuss what happens if only one party actually cares whether the price is too high or too low, and the other party to the transaction does not. In particular, we will explore how this can happen in the labor market, and what the results are when it does.

In a capitalist economy, it is our freedom to make purchasing choices that allows the "invisible hand" to function. Consumers decide to frequent one newsstand, coffee shop, hair salon, clothing store or restaurant rather than another, because they believe what they get for the price is better in one than in the other. The consumer's "right to choose" is the enforcement mechanism of a capitalistic society, determining which businesses are successes and which are not. It works because the basic desire by consumers to get the most value for the price they pay is so widely shared that it seems to be part of the socioeconomic DNA of a free society.

And it is mirrored in the socioeconomic DNA of merchants and business people to charge as much as they can, as long as they can still sell their product or service and stay in business. That's not surprising either, since the people comprising both groups are essentially the same. Most merchants and business people are also consumers, and – at some point or another – most consumers are also sellers of something, even if only their own labor.

Capitalism and its "invisible hand" only work when there are two opposing sides, each trying to get the "best deal" they can, in each transaction. This applies to buyers and sellers of all kinds, including employers and employees, the buyers and sellers of labor.

But what happens when there are not two opposing parties to the transaction? What if only one party actually cares about the resulting price, and the other does not? Or if the other party does care about it, they do not care nearly as much about it as the first side? In that case the "sweet spot" they arrive at is going to be *a lot sweeter* for one party than for the other. The more one party cares about the price of a transaction and the other one does not, the more likely the resulting price will not be an actual market-clearing price, and the transaction will resemble a "gift" more than an arms-length business deal.

The term "sweetheart deal" is often used to describe such a transaction, where the price reflects one side doing a favor for the other rather than bargaining hard and arriving at a true market price. The laws of supply and demand and the Invisible Hand only apply and work well when both parties to the transactions are independent, and able and willing to act in their own interest. "Acting in their own interest" is another way of saying that they act "rationally," as economists would define that term.

Not surprisingly, an economist would regard a "rational" buyer as one who chooses to pay lower prices rather than higher prices, other things (like quality, etc.) being equal. And a rational seller is one who would choose (again, other things being equal) to charge the highest price they can and still do the deal.

For this to happen in the labor market you have to have both parties – the employer and the employee – behaving "rationally" and trying to get the best deal they can for themselves that still allows the deal (i.e. the hire) to take place.

Fortunately in most hiring situations, whether a mom-and-pop grocery store or a large corporation, these necessary elements – interested, motivated parties on both sides of the transaction trying to get the best deal for their side – are virtually always in place.

In the mom-and-pop store, or any of the millions of single proprietorships and small businesses across the country, you usually have a single owner, family or small group of co-owners running the business directly and keeping a close eye on all aspects of it, especially revenues and expenses. Businesses where that is NOT the case are less likely to be successful, and the data show that about half of all new businesses fail in the first five years.

So it would be the rare small business owner who can afford *not* to focus closely on costs, and labor costs typically receive intensive scrutiny. Few small business owners are interested in paying their employees more than they have to. This does not mean that employers are short sighted, or don't want high quality, loyal employees. In that sense it would be totally rational for an employer to pay its workers $15 per hour, even if the typical rate in the local labor market was $13 per hour, if it knew the extra $2 would give them the pick of the crop of employees and ensure a loyal workforce that would make the business successful. But having determined the appropriate margin needed to attract the higher quality workers was $2, it would not be rational to pay them, say, $10 more. To knowingly pay so much more than the amount dictated by the market and the employer's own common sense would not be normal, or make economic sense.

So if we saw a situation where the going rate for a job was $13 per hour and the high end of the scale (if you wanted the very best candidates) was $15 or even $16, and there was a business paying someone $22 or $25, what would we likely conclude? Most likely it would be a case where one party to the "bargain" was not as eager as the other one was to make the best deal that they could. In a small family business it might mean there was a family member (son, daughter, niece, nephew) that the boss wanted to help out or subsidize by paying them at an above market rate.

That, of course, is totally legal and ethical, as long as it's your own company and the "sweetheart deal" you're giving someone comes out of your own pocket. But we should not confuse that with *rational economic* activity. The employer in this case, by consciously deciding to pay the employee more than the free market would require them to pay to obtain the employee's services, is giving a *gift* to the employee of the difference between the market rate of $15 and the actual rate of $22 or $25.

As we said, nobody would quibble or find it irrational to pay a reasonable premium over the market average in order to obtain and retain the highest quality employees available. It is only when the differential becomes inexplicable that it also becomes economically questionable, and we would begin to look for reasons to explain why the normal free market bargaining process has gone awry.

Of course, besides being questionable from an economic standpoint, the above situation is not honest or ethical if the employer does not own the company. Giving a friend or family member a "sweetheart deal" paid for **with somebody else's money** and without their knowledge and approval is akin to theft or fraud, and is generally illegal.

Since this is not a novel, we don't have to worry about "giving away the plot," so readers can probably see already where we are headed with this line of thinking. In most corporations, there are checks and balances and other policies and procedures that encourage or require managers and decision-makers to take actions that conform to basic economic principles.

In other words, goals and performance standards, operating measurements and rewards for most employees and managers throughout the organization are set up in a way that encourages productivity and expense control, whether the expenses being controlled are labor costs or other expenditures. So "the system" works to ensure there are the necessary and motivated "two parties" to the transaction all the way up the corporate ladder. *Until you get to the very top.*

In the next chapter we will examine more closely how operating standards and built-in economic motivators work for most corporate transactions, including decisions about compensation. We will also see how and why they cease to function at the boardroom and CEO level.

Then in later chapters we will discuss the dangerous downside to all this. How having an elite leadership group at the top of the economic pyramid whose pay is not determined by the same "rational" economic principles that apply to everyone else distorts economic decisions, and leads to results that are inconsistent with, and politically dangerous to, a free market economy.

CHAPTER 4

CORPORATE PAY PRACTICES:
BOTTOM TO TOP

Most corporations have institutionalized free enterprise decision-making throughout the organization. A typical corporation is structured like a pyramid, with smaller departments at the bottom reporting up the line to managers of larger and larger ones as you approach the top. Each unit manager has an incentive to maximize revenues and minimize expenses in his or her department.

In other words, they are motivated to engage in "rational" economic behavior as we defined that term earlier. That means they would want to maximize revenues and minimize expenses by negotiating hard and not doing "sweetheart deals" with customers and suppliers. They would also want to pay whatever salaries they had to pay to obtain quality employees, but would have every incentive not to overpay, in order to keep a lid on costs.

Besides their personal self-interest in maximizing the bottom line of their own business units, corporate managers are also steered toward making "rational" purchasing and hiring decisions by:

- Corporate purchasing departments that establish purchasing and procurement policies to ensure competitive bidding and transparent price determination, and

- Corporate human resources departments that provide policies and specialized recruiting staff to ensure professional and consistent practices in hiring and compensating both new and existing employees.

The purchasing department's purpose is to ensure that purchases are made in an arms-length manner at prices that reflect the market and do not disadvantage the corporation. The same is true of human resources departments. Most HR departments are highly professional and work closely with their internal management clients to help them hire, train and retain the employees they need to meet their strategic goals. The HR department's job includes making sure the company "gets what it pays for" when it hires people, which means paying a competitive salary, but not overpaying.

Corporations avoid the sort of "sweetheart deals" mentioned earlier by prohibiting conflicts of interest in both their purchasing and their hiring. To this end, companies have specific rules to either outlaw, or at least control and monitor, any purchases from vendors that are related to the corporate managers doing the purchasing. Similarly on the recruiting side, companies often have nepotism rules that restrict a manager's hiring of family members. All of these rules are intended to avoid conflicts of interest and to ensure that managers are motivated to bargain for the best deal they possibly can on behalf of their company.

Beyond nepotism rules restricting the hiring of relatives, managers get lots of positive assistance in recruiting new employees. Professional recruiters within the HR department generally perform the role of consultants to line managers with positions to fill. Depending on the uniqueness or importance of the position, they sometimes hire outside recruiters (so-called "headhunters") to identify candidates.

In virtually every instance, the recruiter (whether inside the HR department or from the outside) plus the hiring manager will carefully discuss and agree on the job description and the compensation parameters before beginning the search for candidates.

While every company has different practices, a common theme is that every hiring decision and every determination of how much to compensate an employee generally takes place within a framework of policies, procedures and salary guidelines. Besides these formal policies, employment and pay decisions also have several sets of eyes on them – local management and human resources staff involved in the process or monitoring it closely. And every set of those eyes belongs to someone whose job is to manage some aspect of the corporate bottom line, and to make sure the company gets what it is paying for.

That's how it works, *until you get to the executive suite*.

When it comes to setting the compensation for the CEO, there are several critical differences compared to how the pay for everyone else in the corporation is determined:

1. CEOs do not have a specific boss responsible for determining their pay.

2. Responsibility for setting the CEO's pay is usually shared by a subset of the board of directors called the compensation committee that is made up mostly of other CEOs whose own compensation is set in a similar manner by their own boards.

3. The frame of reference for the Board of Directors, in general, is the overall performance of the corporation. So the CEO's pay, no matter how large, is a relatively small expense in relation to total corporate earnings.

4. Recommendations to the compensation committee are typically made by an outside consultant, an expert in executive compensation ("executive comp") hired by the board in collaboration with the company's HR department.

5. Executive comp consultants rely heavily on the recommendations of satisfied clients (i.e. CEOs whose compensation

packages they have designed) in finding new clients.

6. As a result, executive comp consultants have every incentive to recommend boosting the CEO's pay, and very little incentive to question the need for new or additional executive comp programs.

7. There is nobody involved in the CEO compensation process with any incentive to question whether a proposed level of compensation is necessary or excessive.

8. In other words, nobody "sitting at the bargaining table" actively representing the company or its shareholders.

If you deliberately wanted to design a system that thwarted the operation of normal economic principles – like supply and demand, the "invisible hand," equilibrium pricing – it would be hard to find a more perfect one than the CEO compensation model. Virtually all those "checks and balances," the incentives and policies that keep normal corporate managers on the straight and narrow when spending the company's money, are missing when it comes to setting CEO pay.

First of all, there is nobody guarding the henhouse except the foxes, in this case corporate directors whose own pay is determined in a similar fashion and who have a vested personal interest in seeing corporate CEO pay levels increase generally.

The board members most responsible for setting CEO pay are the chairman and other members of the compensation committee, virtually all of whose pay is determined by similar compensation committees back at their own boards.[5]

Just in case any board members were to have qualms of conscience or other

---

[5] In the past, company CEOs often sat on each other's compensation committees and literally set each other's pay. When the author was head of human resources at the Bank of Boston Corporation in the 1980s, the bank's chairman William Brown and General Cinema Corporation's chairman Richard Smith sat on each other's boards and compensation committees and thought nothing of it. Now most companies avoid the practice because it appears to be (and, of course, is) such an obvious conflict of interest. In a real sense, the conflict still exists because board of directors and compensation committee members all have a common interest in preserving the same executive compensation system, whether or not they sit on each other's specific boards or comp committees.

reservations about spending millions more shareholder dollars than are necessary to attract, retain or motivate their company CEO, there are the executive compensation consultants. Executive comp consultants conveniently fill the role of "outside expert" in the process, submitting elaborate reports to assure compensation committee and board members that the proposed compensation is competitive and appropriate. Having a supposedly "objective" outside expert opinion helps assuage any concerns individual board members might have that a pay package is too generous. And board members have a vested interest in being assuaged of that, since they have their own compensation committees and executive comp consultants[6] back home on their boards devising similar pay packages for them.

So any board member who raised concerns about the pay of the CEO at an outside board he or she sat on would be inviting similar objections to be raised about their own pay back at their home company's

---

[6] They are often the same consultants.

board. (Not to mention that they wouldn't be welcomed onto too many other boards.)

Executive compensation consultants put a veneer of legitimacy and validation on what is a giant conflict of interest at the board level. The consultants are hired by the CEOs, although the CEOs typically have their human resources heads do the formal engagement. All parties to the engagement know exactly what the consultant's purpose is. Once engaged, they talk to the company CEO and determine what other firms the company should regard as its "peers" for compensation purposes. (Generally not companies that pay their CEOs *less* than the client company.) Then the consultant goes out and collects information about what the peer companies pay their top officers, along with whatever other market information they deem relevant. After that they come back and deliver their recommendations to the compensation committee of the board. These will usually include pay raises or new bonus or incentive programs to bring the company's CEO and other top officers into what has been determined is the appropriate range of their peer companies.

The use of consultants and the recommendations they make effectively absolves individual board or compensation committee members of responsibility for doing independent thinking, or asking the hard questions one would normally ask before spending tens of millions of dollars of someone else's (the shareholders') money. This allows directors to avoid the difficult, embarrassing questions that they wouldn't want anyone on their own board to ask about their compensation:

- Why are we increasing our CEO's pay to, say, $15 million when he/she already makes $12 million?
- What is the additional value we expect to get? Will they work harder? Be more creative?
- Do we have or have we ever had a problem of CEOs being hired away from us?
- Do we expect to lose our CEO if we don't raise the pay like this?
- How does this increase compare, percentage-wise, with typical pay increases throughout the company?
- In particular, why are we raising the CEO's pay by 25 percent when the

budgeted pay increase for the company as a whole is only 4 percent?[7]

These questions seldom if ever get asked. With the executive compensation consultant's "expert" report in hand, the directors are covered.

The reports that the consultants make to the compensation committee and to the board are their principal way of marketing themselves to other CEOs in order to get new assignments. A consultant that comes across as aggressive and imaginative in identifying reasons why a particular CEO is underpaid relative to his/her peers, and in devising programs to close the purported gap, is likely to get additional assignments.

On the other hand, imagine a consultant that was honest in pointing out that the client hadn't had a CEO hired away in decades and that the current CEO was

---

[7] There is often a big disconnect between the annual percentage increase in the CEO's pay and the budgeted pay increase for the company's employees overall. One would expect the question to arise how the productivity of the CEO manages to continually increase so much faster than the productivity of the rest of the company's employees, so as to justify such a constant gap in percentage increases.

already paid generously and appeared in no danger of jumping ship and moving elsewhere. Or questioned how much extra value the company would receive if it added an additional $3 or 4 million to the CEO's already generous $10 million package.

These are all obvious questions, and certainly ones we would ask if we were hiring somebody to work in our own company and paying them with our own money. But in a corporate boardroom setting they are not likely to be asked, because it is not in the interest of the consultants to ask them, if they want to get hired by other companies. Nor is it in the interest of the HR department head or other compensation professionals within the company to ask them, if they want to keep their own careers on track.

In fact, these questions have not been asked for decades, which is why CEO pay has risen so much faster than ordinary workers' pay for the past half century. To put that in perspective, from 1965 to 2013 average CEO compensation grew by over 1,700%, from $800 thousand to $15 million. During that same period, private sector non-supervisory workers' average pay increased by only \$13,000 from \$39,000 to \$52,000. That's 33% spread over more than 45 years, or virtual stagnation in lower level wages, versus CEO pay growing by over 17 times.

Another way to look at this is that CEO pay was 20 times a typical lower level worker's pay in 1965, and now the gap has multiplied 15 times, to a pay gap of almost 300 times that same worker's pay.[8]

There are two possible explanations for this. One is that CEOs are now 15 times more productive than their lower level employees than they were 45 years ago, and that the requisite talent and skill set needed to be a CEO is relatively 15 times more rare and difficult to find in the job market today than it was back then.[9]

The alternative explanation is the one we have been suggesting, that supply and demand and other free market economic forces that serve as a brake on pay increases are alive and well in the part of the economy where most workers operate; but that these

---

[8] Data from Economic Policy Institute, *Issue Brief #380*, June 12, 2014.

[9] If so, that would be a sad commentary on all the colleges and business schools and the tens of millions of graduates they have pumped out over the decades.

free market forces are essentially "missing in action" in the boardrooms where CEO pay is set. Why have free market forces been effectively banned from the boardrooms in the setting of CEO pay? Because of the inherent conflict of interest in having a group of people determine its own compensation, paid for with other people's money (i.e. stockholders of their companies) without any effective outside controls. In other words, in economic terms, without an actively engaged party on each side of the transaction.

So which explanation is it? Are CEOs so talented and in such short supply in relation to the demand for CEOs that qualified candidates can only be attracted if offered multi-million dollar pay packages? Despite the millions of middle management professionals apparently ready and willing to move up into executive jobs?

Or does our free market labor economy just break down and cease to function when it reaches the executive suite?

I hope, if you've read this far, that the answer to that question is pretty obvious. What is not so obvious is how much our national habit of overpaying our chief executives is actually hurting our economy. Many people recognize that CEOs are way overpaid and that the compensation system is flawed, but just sort of accept it, the way they do hurricanes, epidemics and other natural disasters. "Okay," they say, "a bunch of people who don't deserve it become filthy rich. Well so what, isn't that just life?"

It may be "life" but it isn't the way our free enterprise economy is supposed to work. Accepting it and allowing it to continue costs our society a great deal. It isn't just that corporate executives are being paid grossly more than they otherwise would if the same rules applied to them that apply to everyone else.

It is that the system that rewards them unduly also ***encourages them to make decisions that may be good for them and their pocketbooks, but not necessarily good for their companies and for the economy as a whole***. In chapters to come we will examine this downside, and see that there is even more at stake here than just wasting billions of dollars of shareholders' money.

CHAPTER 5

HOW DID WE GET HERE?

We just noted how CEO pay has gone up about 1,700% over the past 45 years, while rank-and-file pay has gone up by only 33%. After tax, CEO pay has gone up at an even faster rate, since marginal tax rates above $200,000 were as high as 90% in the 1950s, and 70% in the 1960s, before dropping to below 40% since the 1980s.

The gap is even more startling during certain more recent periods. In the five years from 1995 to 2000, CEO compensation soared from $5.7 million to $20 million, a jump of nearly $15 million, or about 250%. During that same time, rank-and-file workers' pay went up by $2,300 from $45,600 to $47,900, or about 5%.

CEO pay took a dive during the financial crash, like everyone else's, as bonuses and stock options took big hits. But since the end of the recession in 2009, while lower level workers' pay has stagnated along with that of typical middle-management professionals, CEO pay has leaped ahead by 50%, from $10 million in 2009 to $15 million by the end of 2013.

So the economic forces, the laws of supply and demand, that have been at work slowing the upward movement of the pay of ordinary workers, have done little to dampen pay increases at the top of the corporate pyramid.

Ordinary workers, of course, have been affected by the globalization of labor markets over several decades. Once employers realized they could outsource jobs to third-world countries with wage rates a fraction of what they are in the United States, it removed the bargaining power of millions of US workers. Moreover, it meant that a worker in Michigan or Pennsylvania or wherever was now effectively competing in the same labor market with workers in India, Bangladesh and China. Even for workers whose jobs have not been moved to offshore locations, the change from a manufacturing-based economy to one based more on services has had a dampening effect on wages for millions of people, especially those unable to transition to the so-called "knowledge worker" category.

Many of today's families in America's industrial heartland had parents and grandparents making steel and automobiles for salaries and benefits of $40 and $50 an hour. Now the current generation is as likely to be serving fast food at $10 or $12 an hour in McDonalds and Chipotles.

So the "iron law of wages" is very much alive in the US economy today, for entry-level and low-skill workers. Even knowledge workers, in what were once called "white collar" jobs prior to the introduction of business casual dress, have felt the downward pressure on wages, especially since the great recession of 2008. Many professionals fortunate enough to have kept their jobs through the crash saw greatly diminished salary increases and bonuses in the years afterward, as the economy and labor markets have struggled to recover.

But it's quite a different story in the executive suite, where free enterprise and the normal effects of supply and demand seem to have "gone missing" in the determination of CEO pay, for reasons we identified in the last chapter:

- Sweetheart deals – Nobody representing the company's shareholders with any incentive to negotiate the lowest possible price; but plenty of people involved in the process (like other board members and consultants) who have personal incentives NOT to negotiate hard or question the need for excessive awards.
- Conflicts of interest – Boards of directors with a vested interest in the outcome, since the CEO pay level and process for setting it at one company become precedents for determining other directors' pay back on their boards.
- Price-fixing – The same executive comp consultants advising multiple boards, along with inter-locking board memberships, serve to maintain a system of inflated compensation levels unrelated to any external supply, demand or market cost of executive talent.

This last factor is never referred to as "price fixing" in polite corporate society. But it bears a strong resemblance to when companies get together, compare notes and agree to prop up the wholesale or retail prices of their products. All of which, of course, is illegal.

Unfortunately, given the lack of effective controls on executive pay, the CEO community can pay itself almost anything it wants, under the current system. So absent any new legislation, regulation or substantial raising of consciousness among shareholders, regulators and the public, the only potential brake on CEO pay is the attitude of the CEOs themselves toward their own compensation.

This is where there has been a major shift in recent decades, as generations of new CEOs have been promoted to boards (their own and others) and introduced to the CEO compensation system, with its surveys, consultants, and the "keep up with the Joneses" approach to continually matching the higher pay of so-called "peers." As a result of years of exposure to all this, most CEOs actually believe they deserve what they are being paid. They have become so steeped in the system and heard so many consultant presentations about what their self-defined peers – i.e. other CEOs – are paid, that it is inevitable they have come to believe that their own pay is reasonable.

And compared to other CEOs' pay, their own pay *is reasonable*. That's the problem. Boards of directors, compensation committees and executive compensation consultants all basically compare notes among themselves to see who is paid how much, and then they compare that with their own pay or the pay of other CEOs in the selected peer group and adjust their CEO's pay to bring it up to or even ahead of the average. The result is a closed system that continually ratchets up everyone's pay, without regard to whether the increases are economically required to attract potential CEO candidates.

But economics is not supposed to be a closed system where people all compare notes about what previous prices for things were and then automatically increase the price from there. In a real economy corporations would be constantly tapping the market for executives and would be paying enough, but no more than necessary, to attract the CEOs and other top executives they needed.

If excessive CEO compensation actually reflects the absence of normal economic forces rather than a genuine market shortage of people with unusually rare CEO skill sets, then we have to ask the obvious question: How did we get to this point?

Forty or fifty years ago CEOs were paid well, but were not paid nearly as much in comparison to everyone else as they have been in recent decades. How and why did that change? And further, how has the change impacted our economy and our society?

There was a time when CEOs accepted the idea that they should be paid well but not excessively, and there was more of a "fiduciary" attitude toward running a company that belonged to other people (i.e. the corporate shareholders). The author recalls his first job as a young international banker in training at Bank of Boston[10] where the CEO at the time, Roger Damon, was widely admired for having turned down an increase in his own pension because he thought it would be unseemly for a CEO to benefit personally from the board's decision

---

[10] Officially the First National Bank of Boston, with branches around the world, it was commonly called Bank of Boston or, south of the border, Banco de Boston. Eventually acquired by Bank of America.

to increase executive pay while he was chairman. So he took the pension that was already in place and let the augmented plan apply to his successor.

Damon retired in 1971. It demonstrates how much Bank of Boston's and the rest of corporate America's attitudes toward CEO compensation changed in the ensuing years that just 14 years later the Wall Street Journal ran a front-page story about the bank's then current CEO William Brown's behind-the-scenes juggling of his own bonus plan.[11] Although the amounts involved at the time were only in the hundreds of thousands rather than the millions of dollars like today, all the familiar elements of self-dealing, conflict of interest and the disconnect between reward and performance were there in the story.

---

[11] The bank had instituted a new bonus plan the previous year that tied the CEO's bonus and the size of the entire bonus pool to earnings-per-share growth. After a mediocre year, Brown was unhappy with the plan formula's payout for him and his most senior executive colleagues, so he overrode the new plan, boosting bonuses for himself and top-level executives by squeezing bonus awards for the middle management ranks.

But more telling than the specific actions of the CEO and his cronies was that their revelation in the press caused hardly a stir among the bank's directors and shareholders. Corporate management, instead of being embarrassed or apologetic about the incident, only seemed to care about catching whoever leaked the story. To that end an internal witch-hunt ensued, albeit an unsuccessful one.

This episode demonstrates the transition in the view of the role of the CEO that took place across corporate America in the 1980s, where the fiduciary model exemplified by Roger Damon and his generation was replaced by the current "gimme the money" attitude. CEOs began to regard themselves as entrepreneurial barons of a corporate state, who should be compensated as such and where there is no shame in aggressively seeking to maximize one's own personal compensation.

Prior to the 1980s there was a clearly understood difference between people who were running a business they had created personally and people who managed a company that someone else had founded. Company founders like Bill Gates and Steve

Jobs (or Henry Ford and John D. Rockefeller in an earlier era) were expected to reap a major share of company profits, either in the form of pay or dividends, because it was their own company and – at least in part – their own money with which they were compensating themselves.

Corporate managers, including the CEOs, of companies they had not founded and were therefore owned by other people (i.e. public shareholders) were essentially "hired hands." They were very well paid hired hands, and often got rich. But they got rich over time, not all at once. They did not get multi-million dollar annual salaries or huge one-time paydays like today's CEOs.

Because those "old time" CEOs made their money gradually over the course of their careers, they had more of an incentive to take a long-term view about what was best for the company, including its shareholders, customers, employees and community. The interests of the CEO and other top corporate officers, as well as of middle management, were more closely aligned with one another. CEOs were usually promoted from within and were not paid as huge a multiple of the middle managers' pay as they are now.

The single most important factor in changing attitudes about CEO pay, and what hastened the opening of the floodgates with respect to massive CEO payouts, was the rise of the "leveraged buyout" or "management buyout" as it is sometimes called. An LBO or MBO was the buyout of a company or piece of a company by a small group of investors, often including the management of the company, using a relatively small amount of equity that was leveraged with a much larger amount of debt, either in the form of high-yield ("junk") bonds or loans ("leveraged loans") from a group of banks.

The premise behind most of the original buyouts was simple. Local management of a subsidiary or division of a larger corporation would go to their management and tell them that they didn't feel they really had enough incentive as paid employees (i.e. "hired hands") to be as aggressive and creative as they would be if they actually owned the company themselves. Therefore, would their bosses, the senior management of the larger corporation, please allow them to buy their division or subsidiary and set it up as a separate company?

If the bosses said yes, then the managers would find some deep-pocket investors (usually called "private equity" firms) to put up the equity for the venture and a syndicate of investment banks would underwrite the bonds and/or loans that would finance the rest of the purchase. These deals were and still are highly leveraged. There might be four or five dollars of debt for every dollar of equity that is invested. When the dust settled, the original owning corporation would have been paid several hundred million dollars or more and the new company would be owned mostly by the private equity firm and its investor clients, with a small piece (10% or so) going to the managers who organized the deal.

Later on, that "small piece" could end up being worth tens or hundreds of millions of dollars to the management team if the business were successful.

These early management buyouts laid the groundwork and set the precedent for many of the excesses in executive pay that followed over the next few decades. They established a principle, largely unexamined and unproven, that giving management large ownership shares of companies they had no personal role in creating was necessary to motivate them to give their maximum effort to the company and its shareholders.

It is hard to argue with the idea that having senior management own some shares of the company they run helps to align their interests with other stockholders. Of course, so do bonuses tied to earnings growth.[12] But the assumption running through many stock option grants and similar programs is that if a $10 million payoff will motivate greater performance than a mere $5 million award, then a $50 million or $100 million payoff must therefore motivate an even more spectacular performance.

This raises a host of questions, most of them centered on the idea of "How much is enough to motivate an executive?" While I

---

[12] In fact, bonuses tied to earnings growth align the interests of CEOs and shareholders even more closely than stock options, since numerous studies show stock market movements reflect an entire range of factors, most of them outside of management control, whereas earnings growth is more likely to be connected to specific management activity.

might work harder to get an additional $5 million as opposed to merely $1 million or $2 million, how much additional creativity and energy do I have in reserve that I will be able to unlock if the company offers me $10 million or $20 million? Let alone another $100 million? In other words, what is the company getting for the additional millions once they meet a certain threshold?

But as we noted earlier, these questions are not likely to be asked by current boards of directors, nor were they being asked back in the 1980s when these deals first began. By now – thirty years later – there is an almost automatic assumption that an executive pay package should include stock grants or options with huge (i.e. multi-million dollar) payoffs as a matter of course regardless of how necessary such a level of ownership is to motivate the CEO to maximum effort.

The idea quickly spread that corporate finance deals, where corporations and their constituent parts get taken apart, re-engineered and stitched back together, were a particularly appropriate occasion for giving CEOs and other executive officers whopping one-time pay packages. What's more, these "event driven" compensation contracts were typically designed as no-risk deals for the executives. If the venture were a big success the executives would get huge rewards, often in the tens of millions of dollars. But even if the deals were not successful executives usually received consolation prizes ("golden parachutes") of one sort or another, typically also in the millions, that removed any personal downside risk at all.

It is this "asymmetry" that is now a standard feature of CEO pay. The idea that there is lots of upside and virtually no downside to life in the executive suite seems to have become a widely accepted feature of today's business practice.

Nobody doubts that providing executives with an equity stake in the company they manage aligns their incentives with the interests of the shareholders. The issue is how much incentive is necessary to motivate an executive to do what is best for shareholders, and at what point the additional compensation becomes redundant, and a misappropriation of shareholders' money.

One well-known example of apparent compensation "redundancy" is the often-cited case of former ExxonMobil CEO Lee

Raymond, whose final year compensation package before his retirement in 2005, including a lump-sum pension payment, was $398 million. During the 13 years he was CEO, he made a total of $686 million, which was an average of over $50 million per year or $144,573 **per day**. In its proxy statement the company said Raymond's pay level recognized his "outstanding leadership of the business, continued strengthening of our worldwide competitive position, and continuing progress toward achieving long-range strategic goals."[13]

Nobody is suggesting that ExxonMobil did not accomplish a great deal under Raymond's leadership. The question is whether the company was economically required to pay him over $50 million a year to induce him to serve as CEO. Would he have refused the job had the pay been only, say, $20 million? Did anyone on the board of directors make any effort to determine what the maximum amount was that ExxonMobil actually needed to pay to obtain his services?

Raymond does not hold the record for CEO pay packages. Former Walt Disney

---

[13] The New York Times, 4/15/2006

CEO Michael Eisner has been reported[14] to have made close to $1 billion from stock options prior to his retirement in 1997.

Unless you believe that Raymond, Eisner, or any other CEO paid in the hundreds of millions of dollars would have slacked off or failed to perform if they had been paid substantially less, you have to wonder: Why would any company deliberately pay their CEOs so much more than they apparently needed to? Does anyone believe CEOs work harder or are more diligent, creative or protective of shareholders when their companies pay them packages worth four and five hundred million dollars than they would be if they had "only" been paid $200 million? Or $100 million, or even $50 million?

Continuing with Lee Raymond as an example, he worked at Exxon for 43 years, starting in the 1960s when starting pay for most college graduates was in the $10,000 to $20,000 range. Did his board of directors really believe that having worked his way up to the top after a lifetime at the company he

---

[14] Los Angeles Times, 12/4/1997

would jump ship if they only paid him in the tens of millions rather than in the hundreds of millions?

But one suspects nobody asked those questions – for the reasons we discussed earlier – about Raymond's pay or about the pay of Raymond's successor, current ExxonMobil CEO Rex Tillerson, whose annual compensation was $33 million in 2014.[15] Like Raymond, Tillerson is also a lifetime ExxonMobil employee, and presumably not a flight risk. Does anyone believe that if he were paid only $20 million instead of $33 million, or promised a retirement benefit less than Raymond's, that he would be any less dedicated or diligent, or be at risk of leaving?

To close the loop on the issue raised earlier about how over-the-top CEO pay programs reinforce each other from one board to another, let us consider Jamie Dimon, the CEO of JPMorgan Chase. Dimon's board of directors, setting what *Fortune Magazine* recently described as a

---

[15] Up from $28 million in 2013, but down from $40 million in 2012.

"low bar" for assessing CEO performance,[16] has awarded him a pay package of $20 million for each of the past two years. This is in spite of a tenure that has included a number of widely reported scandals and management lapses resulting in billions of dollars in losses and fines paid to the government for various infractions.

The author does not doubt that Dimon is a gifted and experienced leader who is working diligently at a very challenging job. But one wonders – once again – how much additional effort and dedication JPMorgan Chase's shareholders have gotten from Dimon in recent years that they would not have received had they only paid him $10 million instead of $20 million.

But how likely is it that hard questions of that sort were raised by the JPMorgan Chase board's compensation committee, which is headed by former ExxonMobil CEO Lee Raymond? Having earned an average of $52 million a year for 13 years as CEO of ExxonMobil, how aggressive is Raymond

---

[16] *Jamie Dimon's Pay Package: Wrong for All the Right Reason's,* by Eleanor Bloxham, Fortune Magazine, 5/18/2015.

likely to be in keeping CEO pay costs down at JPMorgan Chase? Or will he regard Dimon's $20 million per year as being on the modest side?[17]

Obviously, putting highly paid CEOs on your own board's compensation committee is a pretty smart strategy for a CEO who wants to be well paid. Can anyone imagine CEOs who are themselves paid in the hundreds of millions of dollars being inclined to "nickel and dime" proposals to pay another corporation's CEO a mere $20 or $25 million? This is what supports the "keeping up with the Joneses" trend in CEO pay.

When one reads through corporate proxy statements today, it is obvious that

---

[17] None of this is intended as a personal criticism of Dimon, Raymond, Tillerson, Eisner or any of the other CEOs who accept the extravagant pay packages routinely awarded throughout the corporate world. The point of this book is that whoever you are – St. Francis of Assisi, Mother Teresa or a corporate CEO – if you engage in a bargaining process with someone on the other side of the table who is indifferent to the outcome, whether in a flea market or in a boardroom, you will end up with a much better bargain (i.e. a sweetheart deal) for yourself than you would receive in an *authentic* economic transaction.

companies are making a real effort to justify their levels of executive pay in a much slicker and more sophisticated way than they did in past years. But most of the verbiage is of the comparative sort, matching their CEO's pay with that of so-called peers and showing that they are somewhere in the middle. There is virtually no discussion of why they or the peer companies have to pay that high a level to begin with. Nor is there any suggestion that the executives would leave or fail to perform if they only got "normal" raises of three or four percent like most of their employees do.

We can only speculate about what might have happened back in the 1980s if corporations had reacted differently when the first set of managers proposed buying out their own business units because, as mere hired hands, they didn't feel motivated enough to be as creative as they otherwise could be. If only their corporate bosses let them buy the businesses, they said, then they would be properly incentivized to do their best work.

Suppose their corporate bosses, instead of saying, "Of course, here, take the company," had responded instead, "Well, that's too bad. Why don't you find another job somewhere else, since we're sure there must be lots of eager managers who would be thrilled to have your job running this business for the generous salary and bonus we are already paying you."

Does anyone reading this actually believe if it were *our very own business* – store, restaurant, factory, whatever – that we would agree to sell it to an employee who was working for us merely because they felt they weren't motivated enough to do their best job for us if they didn't own the business (*our business!*) themselves?

Yet that is what corporate America did, when it began agreeing to the wave of management buyouts that started in the 1980s. That has led to acceptance of the principle that top management deserves, as a matter of course, to own a major piece of the business it runs. This, in turn, has led to the creation of stock option and other equity award programs that have resulted in billions of dollars of American corporations being given away over the years to CEOs, in return for very little marginal benefit to the corporations or their other shareholders.[18]

---

[18] *Why CEO Pay Reform Failed,* James Surowiecki, The New Yorker, April 20, 2015.

CHAPTER 6

"OH, BUT WE HAVE TO PAY
THIS MUCH!"

I went to my 45th college reunion last year and met a classmate who has gone on to be the head of a major business school and sits on numerous boards of directors. I told him my plans to write a book pointing out how basic economic principles had somehow gotten lost in the setting of executive pay, thinking that – as a student of economics and capitalism – he would welcome my ideas.

Perhaps I was naïve to think that he would react positively. In fact, he defended the system vigorously,[19] pointing out that

---

[19] Of course, as head of a business school, he's a part of it too. There are undoubtedly many corporate CEOs on his own board, whose ideas of what is "reasonable" and "appropriate" compensation are influenced by their own experience. This is why the CEO pay at universities and hospitals has undergone a similar ballooning in recent years, way beyond what

the downside risk of a major corporation not filling its CEO position when it became vacant was enormous, and far outweighed the cost of overpaying by a few million dollars. When you combine that sort of attitude – "Hey, it's the CEO so what's a few extra million dollars or so?" – with the natural tendency of CEOs who are themselves overpaid to give similarly excessive pay to CEOs on whose boards they sit, you end up with a recipe for constantly overshooting what a market-determined level of compensation would be.

But let's examine my classmate's theory that the CEO job is so important that boards should be happy to pay more than the economically "natural" price in order to ensure that the job is never vacant. Is this a justification for paying CEOs on a whole different economic basis than the one corporations use when paying for everybody or everything else? Or is it an argument for more competent boards? Boards that do succession planning and have new potential CEOs identified and waiting in the wings in

---

typical hospital and academic administrators would have traditionally aspired to.

case an existing one dies or resigns? That's what we expect companies to do for critical jobs throughout the organization.

What do we think would happen if the lease expired on a corporation's headquarters in downtown Manhattan, Chicago, Los Angeles or Houston and nobody had done any advance planning about renewing it or finding a new location? Wouldn't the company's operations be seriously disrupted? Probably even more so than having to have the president fill in for the CEO if he or she left suddenly. But I'll bet the person in charge of managing corporate real estate doesn't get paid extravagantly like the CEO. Or suppose the pilot and crew of the corporate jet were unavailable. That would probably be more disruptive than if the CEO were missing, but again it is doubtful that they are paid millions of dollars because of that. Instead, the company probably has a back-up plan to cover that contingency.

In fact, there must be dozens of important employees – critical financial, technology and operations officials – without whom the company's operations would be more disrupted than if its CEO disappeared. But just because these jobs are important, the company doesn't throw its normal compensation policies and standards out the window when it hires for them.

This is not to say that CEOs are unimportant, only that just because many people and things are important doesn't mean we overpay for them on an ongoing basis. Instead it means we plan for their potential replacement and build in some redundancy. That's why corporations have "offices of the chairman" with presidents, vice-chairmen, as well as CEOs, backed up by executive VPs and other senior officials, all being groomed and identified as potential successors for the people above them. And many or most of them would be happy – even thrilled – to be promoted to the jobs above them, even for the routine sort of pay increases they had been receiving throughout their corporate careers.

Imagine a typical 45-year old executive VP who started at the company 15 or 20 years earlier at $50,000 or so and has now risen through the ranks to a position where they currently make $750,000 per year. Having spent decades reaching that level, how do you think they would react if the

CEO took them aside and told them they were about to be promoted to the presidency of the company, and if they did well over the next few years they were then likely to become CEO?

Would they insist that they would only accept the promotion if their pay were increased over that time to $10 or $15 million? Or would they be happy to do the job if their pay were gradually increased to "only" $3 million or $4 million?

To put this into some perspective, most anyone who has worked in a corporation in recent years knows that typical salary increase budgets have been modest at most companies, so for quite a few years many good performers have been lucky to receive raises even as high as 5%. So if our young EVP, starting at $750,000 and promoted to president, were to receive a raise of twice that amount – 10% – for each of the next ten years, he'd be rewarded at a rate way ahead of most of the others in his company.

Yet that generous 10% annual increase would bring him to just under $2,000,000 per year at the end of 10 years. In order to bring that same young EVP up to a level of $5 million, still modest compared to many

CEO pay levels, would require us to raise their annual pay at a rate of 21% per year for 10 years.

So it brings us back to our original question. What makes us think young executives climbing the ladder to the executive suite, knowing there are dozens of other young executives with impressive resumes all ready, willing and able to fill their shoes at a moment's notice, would insist on pay increases of 20% a year and higher if they were offered a major promotion? Especially when they knew the rest of their own company and the economy at large were content with pay increases at a low single digit rate?

Do we really believe that young executive, receiving the opportunity of a lifetime, would turn it down or not work hard at it if they thought their annual pay of $750,000 or so was "only" going to increase to $2 million or $3 million instead of $10 or $15 million?

I hope it is obvious to readers by now that the only thing driving and keeping up CEO pay is the fact that other CEOs control the process. All of them, collectively, have a vested interest in maintaining a bloated system that ensures that as a group they continue to be overpaid.

It is not difficult to see how easily new executives become initiated into the process. One can hardly blame young executives selected for advancement into this elite culture, once they see all the goodies laid out before them (big salaries, and even bigger stock option and incentive programs), for not holding up their hands and saying, "Thanks, but I don't really need all this to do the job you're offering me."

Of course they take their place at the table and go along for the ride. Within a few years of being part of the boardroom culture and listening to executive compensation consultant briefings, they will have begun to believe that they and their colleagues actually deserve the grossly inflated amounts that they are paid. That is how the system perpetuates itself.

CHAPTER 7

BUT OUR COMPANY IS SO BIG......
(BESIDES, WHAT ABOUT
BALL PLAYERS?)

Two of the most frequent arguments you hear justifying inflated CEO pay are totally unrelated but equally specious, so let us deal with them in a single chapter.

The first is the "size" argument: that it is somehow natural that a huge company would pay its CEO and other top executives a lot more than smaller companies would. One can see a certain attraction to this argument. In theory if the responsibility is greater and that translates into a more complex and difficult set of challenges to face it could argue for a more unique set of skills and experience that in turn might command a higher price in the labor market.

But this point is valid only to a limited extent. In reality, holding a management position at smaller firms that are less established than major corporate behemoths – with smaller, leaner corporate staffs, less analytical, technical, legal and other support available at the touch of a button – can be more challenging than holding such a position at a really big company.

So to argue that Lee Raymond and Rex Tillerson, as CEOs of ExxonMobil, one of the largest corporations in the world, deserve to make a *multiple* of more ordinary corporate CEOs' pay because their job is that much more difficult or strenuous or challenging is not likely to survive serious scrutiny. More likely, the size of their employer is merely used as an excuse for the outsize pay awards. But can anyone make a case that either of these two men, both lifelong Exxon employees, would have turned down their jobs or performed less diligently if they were only offered a fraction of the hundreds of millions of dollars they are being paid over their careers?[20] In other words, does anyone

---

[20] As noted earlier, Raymond averaged over $50 million per year for 13 years. Tillerson only made $33 million in 2014, having peaked at about $40 million in 2012. One presumes, unless ExxonMobil has changed its pension plan, he is on track for a substantial payoff à la Raymond's when he retires.

believe there was an *economic necessity* for ExxonMobil to pay them that much?

It is the "economic necessity" test that these huge pay packages for executives of mega-corporations fail. Where is the economic necessity to pay someone more than you otherwise would, or more than the market for their services would require, just because the employer happens to be a huge company?

There is nothing in economic pricing theory or the law of supply and demand to suggest that large buyers should pay more than small buyers when they are purchasing the same thing. All corporations, large and small, operate according to the same economic rules when it comes to setting the prices for what they buy and sell, including the labor that they employ.

When ExxonMobil or another huge company goes out and buys cars from Ford Motor they don't pay more per car than a smaller buyer. Nor do they pay more to buy a barrel of oil than a smaller oil company. In the labor market they don't pay any more for their engineers, janitors, file clerks, secretaries, accountants or truck drivers than other companies a fraction of their size.

So why would they pay more for a CEO who does basically the same job? Especially when large firms have such deep reserves of middle management candidates competing for their top positions.

But, some argue, isn't it much harder work running a big company than a small one? Anyone who knows what executives actually do knows the answer to that, which is essentially "No, it is not."

CEOs, especially of truly large corporations, have experienced management teams that run the major operating and support units (research and development, manufacturing, marketing and sales, finance and accounting, technology, strategic planning, operations, human resources, purchasing, etc.). CEOs spend most of their time meeting with their subordinates, reviewing plans and proposals, and approving or disapproving various courses of action that have been proposed by other executives.

At some firms, CEOs engage in lots of public relations, marketing and interaction with clients. At others the CEO's role may be more internally focused. But in virtually all cases, by the time decisions get to the

CEO level they have been thoroughly reviewed and analyzed by executive staff and other experts.

Many believe that running a smaller, more dynamic, growing company is actually harder work than running a more mature corporation since the management infrastructure – support staff of all kinds – is generally less developed and organized than in a bigger, well-established firm. So CEOs of smaller, growing firms invariably have less professional staff at their side to help them make day-to-day decisions than the CEO of a huge firm.

Okay, you say, but what about baseball players and other professional athletes. Don't they routinely get paid big bucks? Isn't the job of running a major corporation at least as important as playing baseball, football, tennis or basketball? This is a question that CEOs and their defenders often raise when their big paychecks are criticized. Just like the "big firms should pay more than small firms" argument, this one does not stand up to analytical scrutiny either.

First of all, it has nothing to do with which job is more "important." Economics doesn't look at what is "important" or "unimportant."[21] It looks at how "the market," when it is allowed to operate, prices various things, including the jobs people do.

As noted earlier, the market tends to price things based on how scarce they are in relation to how many buyers there are that want to purchase them. So the argument that CEOs of corporations deserve to make as much or more than professional baseball or football players assumes that CEOs have attributes and skills that are just as unique and difficult to find as the skills those professional athletes exhibit. Let's take a look at the facts.

With 30 teams, each with a roster of 25 players, that means there are 750 people capable of playing major league baseball at any one time. Most teams divide the roster pretty evenly between pitchers and other position players, for whom hitting is a prerequisite. That means of 750 players, about 375 of them have to be able to throw over 90 miles per hour and consistently hit

---

[21] If it did, plumbers, teachers and EMTs would probably all make more than CEOs.

the strike zone or a portion thereof. The other 375 have to be able to hit those 90-plus mile-per-hour pitches as well as field a position at a major league level.

It seems pretty obvious that there are a lot fewer people who can either throw accurately or hit successfully a 90 mile per hour pitch than there are qualified candidates to run major corporations. Major league baseball teams have scouts out all over the country monitoring minor league, college and other semi-professional baseball programs, constantly looking for the player capable of joining the majors and ousting one of the 750 players already there. Any major league baseball executive or manager will tell you that finding people good enough to play in the major leagues is very difficult.

By comparison, corporate America is brimming with potential senior executives. Colleges and business schools produce millions of graduates and the professional and middle management ranks of most corporations are filled with top management candidates. To suggest that corporations have anywhere near as much trouble filling their management ranks as major league baseball clubs do fielding a team is hardly credible.

Yet the average major league player's salary is about $5 million, much less than the average CEO's compensation. The players' average is pulled up by the half dozen or so on each team who make true "CEO-level" pay, but the typical player makes less than the average, and over one-third of all major league ballplayers (about 9 or 10 players out of each 25-man roster) earn about $500,000 or less, which may be the pay of a middle-management executive at many companies, but is hardly that of the CEO.

When you consider that even those lower paid players have a set of skills – hitting or pitching at a major league level – scarcer than those of a typical CEO or senior corporate executive, it would appear that the ballplayers are the ones relatively underpaid relative to the CEOs, not the other way around.

This same pattern is repeated in professional football, where a handful of players on each team make "big money" by corporate executive standards, and a typical player makes less than a million dollars. Professional basketball has a lower average salary, just above $3 million, although it has less dispersion around that average (fewer highs and lows), so your typical player is more likely to earn $2 million rather than $500 thousand to $1 million like your typical baseball or football player.

So whichever major professional sport you examine, the average player does not make as much money as the average CEO, even though it seems obvious that the skill set of a professional athlete is more unique than the skill set of most CEOs. In a rational economic market we would expect professional athletes to be earning more than CEOs, rather than less.

Why don't they? The answer is obvious. The market for setting athletes' pay is a *true, competitive market*. Athletes and their agents sit down and negotiate pay with the owners of the teams. Owners of sports teams are not out to waste money. They have no desire to pay any more for a player's services than is necessary. So unlike CEO compensation deliberations, when athletes' pay is negotiated, the people on both sides of the table are actually engaged in hard bargaining.

Unlike most CEOs who have no other company waiting in the wings to hire them away, professional athletes often do have other teams they can move to if their own team doesn't want to pay them sufficiently. That means athletes bring more real bargaining leverage to the table than a typical CEO would (if CEOs actually had to bargain with anyone). But CEOs get paid more than professional athletes in spite of that.

The way athletes' pay is negotiated is a clear example of how CEO compensation is NOT negotiated. In an athlete's contract negotiation there are people sitting on both sides of the bargaining table trying to get the best deal for themselves. This key element of an authentic free market transaction is, of course, lacking in the CEO pay process.

Let us try to imagine what professional athletes' contract negotiations would look like if they followed the CEO compensation model instead of the actual economic model that currently exists for setting baseball or football players' pay.

The player and his agent would still be there pounding the table trying to get paid as much as possible. But instead of having a hard-nosed owner and general manager on the other side of the table, the player and his agent would be negotiating with a group of baseball (or football or basketball) players from other teams.

Of course, all of those other players would know that when it came time to renew their own contracts they'd be sitting down to negotiate with a similar group of other players. So none of them would have any incentive to get too tough or hard-nosed in their negotiating, unless they wanted other players to be similarly tough and hard-nosed with them when it was their turn to re-negotiate.

While this scenario may be mythical (not to mention ridiculous) as far as the negotiation of professional athletes' contracts, it describes perfectly what goes on in CEO pay negotiations. Directors setting CEO compensation are in the same position ballplayers would be in if the players were the ones setting each other's pay instead of the team owners.

Sports fans should be glad players' pay is NOT determined the way corporate CEO pay is. If it were, player salaries would be much higher, and tickets to major sporting events would be even more expensive than they already are.

CHAPTER 8

VICTIMLESS CRIME?
HARDLY!

Many people who are personally unhappy at the level of CEO pay still tend to shrug it off as just another aspect of an unfair or corrupt system that we can't do anything about. They also tend to minimize its negative effects. "Hey, so what if there are rich people who don't actually deserve it. What else is new?"

This cynical attitude, unfortunately, is shared by the power elite that could, if it wanted to, actually do something about it. In 1990 the author, in the midst of one of several career "reinventions," was a journalism student at New York University and wangled an invitation to the annual dinner of the New York Financial Writers Association. The guest speaker was Richard Breeden, then chairman of the US Securities & Exchange Commission. During the question and answer period after his speech, Mr. Breeden was asked what the SEC's position was on the conflict of interest represented by having CEOs sit on each other's boards and set each other's pay. He read the question, thought for a second, and then looked up and laughed. He made no attempt to answer it or even take it seriously, treating it like it must have been a joke. Then he moved on to the next question.

I do not remember anything else Breeden said that evening 25 years ago, but will never forget that question and the non-answer it evoked. I remember thinking at the time, "If that is how little importance the chairman of the SEC attaches to this issue, then we are in for a lot of trouble as a country and an economy."

Twenty-five years later the problem of CEO pay and the outdistancing of the pay of ordinary workers by the incomes of the very rich has become more serious than ever. The problem isn't that people are getting "too rich." Remember, in a capitalistic system there is no such thing as "too rich" in an economic sense, as long as people earn their wealth honestly and in conformance with the rules of the free market. It is in the nature of a competitive society and a free enterprise economy that there will be winners and losers, and that many of the winners will get rich.

The problem even goes beyond the fact – serious though it is – that in consistently overpaying CEOs boards of directors have misallocated billions of dollars in shareholder wealth.

Readers seeking more details of this should check out *Pay Without Performance: The Unfilled Promise of Executive Compensation,* by Lucian Bebchuk and Jesse Fried, of Harvard and University of California Law Schools, respectively, and *Indispensable and Other Myths: Why the CEO Pay Experiment Failed and How to Fix It,* by Southwestern Law School's Michael Dorff. Both books explain in great detail just how ***bad a bargain*** shareholders have gotten for what they have paid their corporate leaders.

But the problem goes much deeper than the mere fact that there have been thousands of "bad bargains" struck between CEOs and the companies that employ them. As we have seen, the real problem is that there is **no bargain** in most CEO pay "negotiations" because nobody is doing any bargaining. Neither the board of directors nor anyone else is actively representing the owners of the company in negotiating pay with the CEO and other top officers.

Free enterprise can tolerate bad bargains once in awhile. Windfall profits and losses, and just plain old "bad deals" are a normal part of the economic game. But exorbitant CEO pay is more than just an *occasional* bad deal for stockholders.

We have **institutionalized a bad deal for stockholders** by completely removing normal free enterprise economics from the executive pay-setting process.

Think about what this means. *The corporate leadership class in the United States, the largest capitalist economy in the world, has disconnected its own compensation, motivation and rewards from the operations of the free market.* For this our society is paying a heavy price.

What price, you ask? It isn't merely the undeserved compensation. If it were just a whole bunch of people getting rich who didn't actually deserve it, that would be less harmful. But the "motivation" part of it is what is so damaging to our economy and our society. Unfortunately this has gotten very little attention.

Back when CEOs were paid generous but not excessive amounts (one or two million dollars instead of fifteen or twenty million, for example) and huge lump sum payments, "golden parachutes" and similar windfalls had yet to appear on the scene, CEOs tended to focus more on the longer-term health of their company. CEOs still became rich but their wealth accumulated over time rather than all at once. Having less of a gap between the chief executive's compensation and that of middle management and other employees served to align the CEO's interest with that of his (or her) co-workers, as well as that of shareholders, customers, suppliers and others with a stake in the company's long term success.

Even with more modest pay, there was never any shortage of qualified candidates for CEO and other top corporate positions, which is evidence that the price the labor market at the time was setting for executive talent was adequate.

The "big bang" approach to CEO pay – huge payouts often connected with major events like mergers and acquisitions – has drastically altered the balance between:

- Managing for the long-term good of the company and its constituents, and
- "Betting the farm" on mega-deals of one sort or another that will pay off in the short term, especially for the executives that organize and execute the deals (and their advisors in the investment banking community).

If a CEO has a choice between (1) accumulating, say, $25 million over the course of a lifetime by guiding and nurturing a company for many years, or (2) doing a single deal that may end the company as employees, customers and constituents know it but lets the executive earn the whole $25 million all in one fell swoop, it becomes an easy choice for many CEOs to take the money and run. The more this has become the norm in recent decades, the less pushback CEOs get from boards or others when they propose it, since everyone else is doing it or has hopes of doing it (including the other CEOs on their board).

What makes the practice even more "non-economic" in a free market sense is that when we say the CEOs are "betting the farm" it isn't even their own farm that they are betting. As noted earlier, except in rare cases like the Messrs. Ford, Rockefeller, Hewlett, Packard, Jobs and Gates where the original CEOs created the "farms" that they were running, 99% of CEOs are mere hired hands on the farms they are running (and betting). So when they do the mega-deals that pay off so handsomely for themselves, they are actually betting and putting at risk someone else's farm (the shareholders'), not their own.

Imagine if you could go into a Las Vegas casino and bet all you want with your rich uncle's or someone else's money, and you got to keep a portion of any winnings, but if you lost it all, well, *they – **not you*** – took the loss. You would have an incentive to play the riskiest games with the biggest payoffs, since if you lost it wouldn't be your problem, but if you won you'd be on easy street.

Does that sound like a good deal? Wait, it gets better. Suppose after you lost all your uncle's money, instead of just sending you away, he said, "Hey, I feel badly that you devoted your time to betting (and losing) so much of my money that I want to give you a gift on the way out the door. Please take this $10 million with you so you won't feel so bad."

That's pretty much the deal CEOs get when they do these mega-deals with their shareholders' companies. If it pays off they get huge personal payouts. If it doesn't work out and the board decides to fire them, they usually get exit packages ("golden parachutes") in the multi-million dollar range. Of course this is in marked contrast to how middle management and the rank-and-file in these companies get treated in the same transactions. If they are lucky, they may get to keep their jobs in the post-mega-deal organization, or they may even get a severance package if they lose their jobs and have been with the company for many years. (Generous severance packages for the middle management or rank-and-file might mean 3 to 6 months of pay, but nothing comparable to the sort of packages CEOs get if they lose their jobs.)

Why do boards and compensation committees go along with such outlandish deals for the CEOs? As described earlier, they have executive compensation consultants telling them it is "the norm" in

CEO compensation. "All the other companies do it," they are told. So they do it as well.

If you are a director in those circumstances, especially knowing the shoe may be on the other foot some day when your company does such a deal and you are eligible for a similar package yourself, it is difficult not to go along with the program. It would be ungracious, and a bit dangerous to your career and compensation prospects, to raise objections or question whether such a large payment was "necessary."

Given the guaranteed payoff for management whether the deals pay off for shareholders or not, you can hardly blame CEOs for trying to do major mergers, acquisitions and other complex transactions, even if the deals have little economic purpose other than to generate bigger pay packages for the corporate executives.

Of course CEOs don't think of it that way. In fact, they don't even come up with the idea for most of the deals that they end up doing. There is an entire industry, the investment banking business, whose purpose is to come up with ideas for potential transactions – usually mergers and acquisitions of one sort or another.

The main goal is to get the deal done (i.e. financed by investors) and, as a result, generate big fees for the bankers and huge payouts for the corporate management involved. If the deal also makes economic sense, that's a plus but not a requirement.

This is why you cannot separate the huge growth in pay for corporate leaders with the explosion of pay on Wall Street. Wall Street has essentially become the "enabler" of the bloated compensation for corporate CEOs.

Young MBAs with corporate databases and Excel spread sheets sit in cubicles in investment banks running programs looking for possible matches of company A and company B, or divisions or operating units of company A and company B. They run financial projections for the resulting merged entities, to see if the projected earnings and balance sheets look reasonably "bankable." In other words, if they can convince the managements of the two companies to merge, will they then be able to persuade investors to finance it? If the answer to all that is yes, then the bankers go out and visit the CEOs of the companies involved and sell them on the idea of merging or having one acquire the other (voluntarily or involuntarily).

They will talk a lot about "synergies" and "shareholder value" but the real incentive – the main reason they are sitting there having the conversation – is that the deal will generate millions of dollars in fees for the investment bankers who dreamed it up, and millions of dollars of bonuses, stock options and "golden parachutes" for the top executives of both companies involved (winners and losers, whether they keep their jobs or not).

Of course, the company has to pay for all this, so it generally comes out of "savings" squeezed out of the resulting company's operations by consolidating plants, cutting staff, moving jobs overseas and other economies that have very real costs for the employees and communities affected.[22]

---

[22] Economists call these "social overhead" costs. They are costs absorbed by the society at large rather than by the persons or companies involved in the transaction. They can run into the hundreds of millions of dollars, and include supporting, re-training and moving unemployed or laid-off workers, the impact of fewer career opportunities on young

This is a total change from the historic roles of both corporate CEOs and their investment bankers, driven by the explosion in compensation on Wall Street and in corporate boardrooms. The effect has been two fold:

- Diverting corporate CEOs' attention away from the longer term strategies that used to motivate them, like nurturing relationships with customers, suppliers, employees and their community, and
- Diverting investment bankers' attention away from their traditional roles of creating relationships with corporate clients and assisting them in developing and executing their own strategies over the long term.

Instead, we have replaced both of those with (1) a CEO class focused mostly on protecting and enhancing its own compensation system, and (2) a Wall Street community focused mostly on "doing deals" that enable the enrichment of its corporate

---

workers, and the negative impact on schools, public services, businesses, local charities and other organizations when factories and corporate headquarters close down.

CEO client base and help justify the bankers' own huge personal compensation.

It is no coincidence that the only part of the economy whose own compensation levels have routinely kept up with the corporate CEO sector has been Wall Street. The two complement each other. Without corporate America going along with thousands of M&A and similar deals whose primary economic rationale is to generate fees, Wall Street's golden egg would tarnish quickly. Meanwhile, the standard Wall Street template for those deals is now well established as one that routinely writes in huge payouts for corporate management whether the deal is a success or not. In this way, both backs are well scratched.

This has become the reality in corporate America and on Wall Street. Deals are done largely to earn fees for the bankers and gross pay packages for the executives. Economic rationales, if there are any, are secondary. The bottom line improvements for the company are often due to closing factories and offices, and laying off employees: actions the management would generally have been less inclined to take if its own interests were more aligned with those of employees and long-term shareholders.

The financial crash of 2007-2008 brought these trends into sharp focus. Library shelves and magazine racks are filled with books and articles about people who ran banks, securities firms, mortgage and insurance companies and other businesses into the ground, but still walked away with hundreds of millions of dollars in compensation.

It is easy to condemn companies like Merrill Lynch, Bear Stearns, Lehman Brothers, Countrywide Financial, Fannie Mae, Freddie Mac, Wachovia, Washington Mutual and others that overpaid their executives just to see the firms crash and burn under their "leadership." But the real point of this book is that even healthy companies routinely overpay their CEOs and incentivize them to do things that are not in the long-term best interest of co-workers, shareholders, customers and constituents.

Think of the difference between CEOs who are "in it for the long run" and compensated reasonably at a level that will make them wealthy over the course of their careers, versus CEOs who are paid at a level that makes them super-wealthy in just a few years and lets them hit the jackpot all at once if they do that corporate mega-deal that transforms the company.

Which CEOs are more likely to care about their local communities and co-workers and to value the relationships they and their companies have established over many years? And which ones will be more inclined to make decisions to outsource jobs, close down plants and take other actions that involve heavy human and other "social overhead" costs without as much regard for the broader corporate constituency?

It is no accident the change in pay practices that has put corporate CEOs in a whole different economic class than their fellow workers has coincided with the move to consolidate companies and eliminate thousands of major manufacturing centers and separate corporate headquarters all across the country. Gone too is the rich tapestry of local business, social and cultural relationships that they supported.

When a corporation's headquarters is in a community, you have the CEO, senior officers, many of the directors and other key employees, as well as the rank and file workers all living there and contributing to the life of the community. Senior officers sit on the boards of local charities. Companies contribute to local schools and colleges, not just because it is the right thing to do, but also because it helps provide a well-prepared work force on an ongoing basis. There are synergies all around, as many of us who grew up in cities across America that housed corporations can attest.

When companies gobble up other companies, typically the plants and office buildings are shut down or downsized. Even if they are not completely eliminated, once it is no longer a corporate headquarters the local community loses the attention – charitable contributions, volunteerism, civic involvement by senior management – that it used to enjoy when it had the people running the company living there as neighbors. Multiply this by countless cities and towns across the country and you see the result of motivating CEOs to "swing for the fences" instead of growing their companies organically over the long term.

The point isn't that doing mergers and acquisitions or "swinging for the fences" is always inherently bad (or good). It is that when we pay CEOs so much more than is economically necessary to get them to do their basic job (i.e. run their company prudently, with a medium to long term perspective), we change their personal incentives, often in a way no longer consistent with the goals of the company's shareholders or broader constituency (employees, customers, suppliers and community).

There is a huge cost to this. Our country has been paying it for several decades, but is only just beginning to appreciate and recognize how substantial the consequences are.

CHAPTER 9

"WE'LL HAVE WHAT THEY'RE HAVING"[23]

In the last chapter we discussed how paying CEOs more than is economically necessary may motivate them to do things that may be good for themselves personally but not necessarily good for their companies, stockholders, employees or communities. It would be like rewarding a quarterback only for completing long passes, rather than for winning games. He might be motivated to throw passes on every play, rather than mix up his plays to actually gain yardage and score touchdowns.

But this problem of "perverse incentives" extends beyond merely motivating CEOs to do things that may not be good for their companies or for society at large. It also sends the wrong message to voters about

---

[23] Special thanks to Estelle Reiner.

what sort of public policies and programs are appropriate if we want our free enterprise economy to be successful. Seeing the sweet economic deal that corporate leaders have given themselves, would it be so unreasonable for voters to decide they wanted a similarly "risk-free" economic balance for themselves, instead of the traditional free market risk/reward paradigm?

Most Americans are not economists, lawyers or compensation specialists. But they are able to figure out basic economic principles, like supply and demand. They know that when the economy contracts or we have a recession many of them lose their jobs; or if they are lucky enough to keep their jobs, their wages tend to stay flat or even be reduced as companies cut back on expenses and try to ride out the economic storm.

They also know that their houses may go down in value, reducing or wiping out their home equity, which for many people accounts for most of their life savings. And if they have stocks in an IRA or 401K plan, they have seen first hand how those values can drop, again reducing their savings and security.

Knowing from experience how classical economic principles apply to ordinary people, Americans accept the downside risks of living in a capitalistic system. Most of us have seen in the lives of our families and friends over many generations that the upside of living in a free economy far outweighs the downside.

Part of the acceptance of the risks, and the virtually universal buy-in to our system by most citizens, is due to our having introduced "safety net" features to limit the economic downside. Programs like Social Security, Medicare and Medicaid, various housing and food subsidies for needy families, all have elements that over time have been politically controversial. But – like them or not – they take some of the "rough edges" off capitalism and have helped our system to sustain political support through the Great Depression and more modest recessions since then when other countries have been tempted to make more drastic changes.

As a result, we have evolved to a balance, politically and economically:

- A free enterprise system where everyone (at least in theory) is subject to the disciplines of the "market,"
- A government that plays the role of "umpire" in enforcing the rules of that free enterprise system, and
- A safety net that provides a minimal level of income, security and medical care to people, even if they turn out to be the "losers" in the competitive free enterprise "game."

Defining how extensive the safety net should be is a controversial political issue and well beyond the scope of this book. The author believes most Americans, whether liberal or conservative, Republican, Democrat or independent, would agree on a minimal safety net level. Achieving political consensus about possible improvements or alterations to the existing safety net, or even how to finance and sustain it going forward, continues to be challenging.

But wherever people may be in that debate, there seems to be a growing recognition by Americans across the political spectrum that a different set of rules and a very different safety net exist for the people at the top of the corporate pyramid than exist for everyone else.

Politicians and commentators often throw around the terms "capitalism" and "socialism." While economists and political scientists have specific definitions for each, I believe that a key difference in many people's minds is captured in the idea that:

- Capitalism connotes the idea of a system where one enjoys the freedom to make economic choices, and to enjoy the upside rewards as well as suffer the downside losses that are the consequences of those choices.

- Socialism, by contrast, suggests a system where one still makes choices, but the scales are tipped more toward the potential upside rewards, with potential downside losses largely mitigated or removed.

If the American people come to recognize that corporate boards and CEOs are operating more of a "socialistic" approach to executive compensation than a free enterprise approach, with (1) all upside and no downside for CEOs and other top executives, and (2) a "suspension" of the law of supply and demand in the setting of CEO pay levels, that will threaten the political balance that has supported free enterprise policies for generations.

If voters see corporate CEOs enjoying a high-level "welfare state" that they have created for themselves where they are protected from the vagaries of normal economic life, then why wouldn't voters want similar protections for themselves? This is an enormous potential political issue, and one that should be just as important to conservatives as to liberals, to Democrats as to Republicans.

If conservatives and other supporters of capitalism want voters to embrace free enterprise policies and a government that interferes as little as possible in the economic sphere, then they need to ensure that our so-called free enterprise economy actually behaves like one, at every level.

Failure to do that is to hand a major issue to welfare state advocates, who will argue that our free enterprise system is a sham, where many of the wealthiest among us have only achieved their riches by gaming the system. Their proposed solution, of course, will be programs to limit incomes and redistribute wealth arbitrarily.

If we expect our capitalistic, free market system to be taken seriously and to command the respect and political support of all of our citizens, then our corporate leadership elite has to show its support and respect for it as well. That requires restoring free market principles to our corporate boardrooms and having CEOs and other corporate leaders face the same balance of economic risk and reward that the rest of us do.

CHAPTER 10

HOW DO WE FIX THIS?

The first step in fixing a problem is recognizing you have one and describing it correctly. We need to reject the idea that excessive pay for CEOs is just a "normal" part of capitalism in the same way that we refuse to accept price fixing, embezzlement and other corrupt activity.

Board members, the SEC, journalists, commentators and especially shareholders need to recognize that paying an executive more than is economically required is a misuse of shareholder assets just as much as any other "sweetheart deal." A class action suit or two by shareholders against boards of directors for breach of fiduciary duty in failing to exercise prudent judgment in approving particularly excessive CEO pay awards might help to raise consciousness on this issue.[24]

As some of the authors previously cited have described in their books, there are many ways to address out-of-control executive pay, once boards of directors decide they want to do so. In particular, there are caps one can put on stock options and incentive plans, so they would "top out" at certain limits.

It is difficult to find anyone who believes CEOs would hold back on their creativity or level of effort if the lottery ticket that paid off when they succeeded was "only" worth $10 million instead of $50 million. In fact, it would be interesting to listen in on the

---

[24] Also helping to raise consciousness may be a new rule, adopted August 5, 2015 by the Securities & Exchange Commission, requiring corporations to disclose the ratio of the CEO's compensation to the median compensation of their employees. Although until now most shareholders have not paid much attention to CEO pay excesses, some experts believe the new disclosures may cause enough outrage in certain quarters that it "may energize a cadre of new combatants in the executive pay fight." ("Why Putting a Number to CEO Pay Might Bring Change," by Gretchen Morgenson, New York Times, August 9, 2015)

negotiation where a CEO explained to his (or her) board what extra level of effort they planned to give if they received that $50 million lottery ticket instead of only the $10 million one. If you were on that board, you might ask your executive recruiter to go out and find some additional candidates who would be willing to give you their maximum effort for just $10 million.

But rolling back or capping executive pay is easy, if boards want to do it. What's required is the act of will. The author is not advocating that we legislate pay limits or interfere directly in the labor markets. What is mostly needed is (1) to educate the public and the investment community about basic economics and how it applies to setting CEO pay, (2) to educate boards about their responsibility to shareholders to see that those economic principles are actually applied, and (3) to enforce these standards through legal and regulatory action.

Most corporations already have human resource and compensation professionals working for them who could show them how to recruit and compensate senior executives, including their own CEOs, in a cost-effective way. They know what questions to ask and could actually serve as internal consultants to their own boards' compensation committees if invited to do so. Here are some important questions that should be asked in every instance:

- Are we recruiting from inside or outside the company? (Most companies promote their senior management from within, and have many capable candidates ready and willing to do the jobs for normal, reasonable pay increases.[25])

- What do we realistically need to pay to encourage this candidate to willingly accept and do the job? What has been his or her salary history within the company up to this point?

- Have we had any CEOs leaving or getting hired away from us because they weren't paid enough? Do we anticipate this problem in the future?

If we got into the habit of routinely asking these basic questions, and educated the public and boards of directors generally

---

[25] If they don't have capable internal candidates, then the board should insist the company create a management development and succession-planning program.

that these are relevant economic criteria in setting CEO compensation, we could begin to create a new climate around executive pay. It would require everyone involved in the process – directors, executives, economists, professors in business schools, shareholders, SEC regulators – to adopt a new mind set about the economic principles that apply to recruiting and compensating our corporate leaders.

This may sound revolutionary in the context of how the executive pay process currently works. But what we are proposing – that the market for executive talent should be negotiated and priced on the same basis that all other wages and prices are set throughout the economy – is NOT particularly radical. What WOULD be truly radical would be a proposal to adopt the system that currently exists.

Suppose our current system of paying CEOs did not exist. Then imagine someone came along and proposed that we pay everybody in the country according to normal free enterprise principles EXCEPT the CEOs, who would be exempt from those principles. Instead, their pay would be set:

- By their cronies behind closed doors,

- With no external market or other controls, and
- The "sky was the limit" in terms of the amounts that could be awarded.

We would look at anyone who proposed that as though they were crazy. Conservatives and liberals – Rand Paul, The Heritage Foundation, George Will, Larry Kudlow, Elizabeth Warren, Paul Krugman, Bernie Sanders, and everyone in between – would all come together to shoot it down because it violated our most cherished economic principles.

Unfortunately, a system like that is already in place. But for the sake of our economy, our democracy[26] and our free society, we need to change it.

---

[26] We have not even addressed the impact of all these newly enriched executives on our political system, where wealth increasingly means power and influence. When we pay those CEOs an extra 40 or 50 million dollars they have not actually earned, we are not just giving them additional homes in Palm Beach or Boca Raton. We are also giving them a disproportionate level of political influence over the nation's affairs at large.

APPENDIX:

THE "CONDENSED VERSION"

The author's goal is to explain to a popular audience in plain English how the CEO compensation system currently works, and to compare and contrast it to how it should work if normal "free enterprise" economic forces were allowed to operate. Equally important, we describe the negative impact on society of exempting our corporate leadership elite from having their own careers exposed to the normal risks and rewards of a capitalistic environment (like everyone else.)

As noted in the preface, some readers will experience an "Emperor's New Clothes" moment upon reading the preface or the introduction, and "get it" immediately. Others may find this "Condensed Version" sufficient, while some will choose to work their way through the entire book. Whatever works. My goal is to have people understand this topic, get excited about it, and go out and demand that something be done about it.

So here it is in a nutshell.

To understand how non-economic our CEO pay practices have become, we first need to spend some time reviewing how prices, including wages, are supposed to be set in a real capitalist (also known as "free enterprise") economy.

Chapter 1 is a refresher course called "Economics 001" that reviews the basics of economics. Most rational people want to pay as little as possible for what they buy, or if they are selling, they want to price it as high as they can. But both of these desires are self-limiting. If I price something too high, few people will want to buy it; and if I offer to pay too little, nobody will want to sell it to me. Some other interesting variations on this theme are that the higher the price of something rises, the more sellers eventually show up trying to sell it for that higher price. (That's called an "increase in supply.") But the lower the price of something falls, the more buyers will show up trying to buy it at the low price (an "increase in demand").

Meanwhile the lower price will discourage sellers, so fewer of them will show up any more to sell it at that low price, and with fewer sellers, the price will eventually go back up; until it gets high enough that it starts to scare off buyers, etc. The effect of all these things happening at once – high prices attracting sellers but scaring off buyers; low prices attracting buyers but scaring off sellers – results in prices of things in a free economy constantly rising and falling, attempting to find an "equilibrium" level. That may last for a nano-second in a fast-moving market (like a stock market) or for days or weeks in more stable markets where the supply and demand don't change so fast (tractors, airplanes, refrigerators, real estate).

In economics these basic rules of human behavior are often referred to as the "laws" of supply and demand. The way in which markets automatically and dynamically respond to changes in price, or to changes in the supply and demand of various things, without any controlling authority telling them to, was labeled "the invisible hand" by Adam Smith, who is credited with having written the first modern book about economics, called *The Wealth of Nations*, in 1776.

In chapter 2 ("Labor Economics 001") we take the basic theory of how prices in general are set in a free market economy and apply it more specifically to how prices for hiring people (i.e. wages) are set. We see the same principles of supply and demand at work, with the "invisible hand" working behind the scenes, helped along by human nature.

People (the "sellers" of their labor), just like sellers of other things, want to be paid as much as they can for the work they do. Employers (the "buyers" of that labor) generally want to pay as little as possible to the people they hire. In general, employers determine how much they need to pay to get the quality of employees they want and/or need, and do not willingly pay any more than that. Even an employer who deliberately decides to pay at the top of the market in order to get the "best of the best" from the local talent pool, will not irrationally pay any more than what is required to achieve that hiring goal.

One key principle from both Economics 001 and Labor Economics 001 is that a rational buyer will constantly be asking, implicitly if not explicitly in their purchasing decisions: How much do I have to pay to buy this item, or – if it's a hiring transaction – how much do I have to pay to induce this person to come work for me? And the assumption, baked into our free market model, is that their goal is to pay that price, or that wage, and no more.

But this "invisible hand" doesn't work all by itself. "It takes two to tango," as we say in Chapter 3, which is our corny way of expressing another key point of economic theory: that for supply and demand and our other economic theories to work in practice there have to be two parties actively bargaining with each other, each one attempting to get the best deal they can get.

If one party is trying to get the best price they can for themselves (highest price if they're selling, lowest price if they're buying) and the other party is only making a half-hearted effort (or worse), then it won't be a true economic transaction and the price arrived at will not be a true "equilibrium" price. Why not? Because it won't be the price they would have arrived at if both parties negotiated hard and in good faith. It will be a "sweetheart deal" where one party agreed to a price that favors the other party, compared to what the price would have been had they both bargained hard. A sweetheart deal is basically a gift – somebody is paying more than they really have to, or selling for less than they really have to – rather than an authentic arms-length economic transaction.

Why is this important? Because while anyone has the right to make all the sweetheart deals they want to with their own money or their own property, nobody has the right to make sweetheart deals (i.e. make a gift) of someone else's money or property (for example, their employers'). That's why a company fires its purchasing agent if they do a sweetheart deal to rent office space at an above market price or buy cars at an above market price from their cousin or brother in the real estate or automobile business.

This "taking two to tango" principle is critical because we come back to it in the next chapter when we examine who (if anyone) is negotiating on behalf of the company and its shareholders in setting the CEO's pay, and whether they are bargaining seriously or just going through the motions in what is just another form of sweetheart deal.

In Chapter 4 we discuss how corporations make decisions about how much to pay for things, including people. For the most part companies have institutionalized rational economic decision-making (i.e. free enterprise) throughout their organizations. They have done this in three ways:

1. Organizing themselves into profit and loss centers so managers are incentivized to scrutinize costs and run their own departments as mini-businesses with their own bottom line that they are responsible for. Managers above them in the organizational structure are motivated to monitor the costs below them, so you have several sets of eyes on every expenditure.

2. Having a purchasing department and purchasing guidelines that set procedures and standards to ensure arms-length dealings with suppliers and avoid the sort of sweetheart deals mentioned earlier, and

3. Human resources departments that manage and monitor the hiring and compensation process, to ensure that salaries and other incentives are within prescribed guidelines tailored to each position level within the company

This makes sure that managers throughout the organization are playing the role they are supposed to, and that the company is getting its money's worth when it makes purchases or hires and compensates people. In other words, it ensures there is someone effectively sitting on the company's side of the bargaining table when these transactions are done.

But all this scrutiny and monitoring disappears when you reach the CEO and board level. Here the CEO's pay is set by corporate directors who are effectively members of a rarified club that has a vested interest – as a group – in seeing the general level of CEO pay continue to rise. Advising the corporate directors on the level of pay that is "competitive" for each CEO are executive compensation consultants who themselves have a vested interest in being perceived as aggressive and creative in getting higher and higher pay packages for their clients.

As a result, at the CEO level, boards of directors go through the motions of having consultant briefings and publishing fancy compensation reports in their proxy statements, but no real negotiation takes place nor are hard questions asked because nobody involved in the process has any incentive to do so.

In Chapter 5 we discuss how we got to this point, and especially how CEO pay managed to jump by 1,700% over a 5-decade period when rank-and-file pay only increased by an anemic 33%. We examine in particular the role that leveraged buyouts in the 1980s played in promoting the concept that management should be compensated like owners, even of companies for which they were mere "hired hands" rather than founders or creators. This ripened into the idea that major corporate events, especially mergers and acquisitions, were occasions when management would be given unusually generous compensation packages. This has had the effect of encouraging CEOs to focus their attention more on doing blockbuster deals than on building their companies organically, as previous generations of more modestly compensated CEOs were inclined to do.

We review, as a classic, often-cited example of alleged CEO compensation excess, the $398 million that former ExxonMobil CEO Lee Raymond received during his final year in office about ten years ago. It is hard for most people to imagine that Raymond, a lifetime Exxon employee, would have turned down the top job if his ultimate reward had been capped at "only" $50 million or $100 million instead of $398 million. Unfortunately we will never know, because, given how CEO pay is set in the corporate world, it would have been unusual if anyone on ExxonMobil's board had actually tried to negotiate down or question the necessity of such a huge payment.

We later observe that JP Morgan Chase's CEO Jamie Dimon is smart to have Raymond on his board and compensation committee. One suspects an executive who received $398 million in his final year ($686 million in total, or $144,573 per day, from 1993 to 2005) may be unlikely to raise too many objections to Dimon's relatively modest $20 million pay package.

In Chapter 6 we examine the argument heard from some directors that the CEO position is so vital that it is well worth overpaying if necessary to ensure against its being vacant, even for a brief period. When you combine this attitude – "Hey, it's the CEO so what difference does overpaying by a few million dollars make?" – with the "keeping up with the Joneses" approach of the executive compensation consultants, you have a recipe for constantly overshooting an economically "necessary" level of compensation.

But how valid is the "pay any price to keep the CEO's chair filled" argument, anyway? There are plenty of other positions in a company whose vacancy would be equally or more disruptive than doing without a CEO for a week or two. Losing your key technology and operations managers, financial and accounting executives, or even the pilot of the corporate jet would likely be at least as disruptive. Yet the company doesn't distort its normal compensation policies in filling these positions. Like the CEO position, these jobs are all very important. But the secret to ensuring they are always appropriately filled is not to overpay, but rather to do succession planning and have potential replacement candidates lined up in advance.

In Chapter 7 we address some other common arguments used to defend inflated CEO pay. The first is that the bigger the company, the harder the job and the higher paid the CEO should be. That is not an unreasonable argument, until you hear it being used to justify paying the CEO of some giant company a grossly inflated *multiple* of what would be economically justified, under any stretch of one's imagination.

Is it a lot harder to run a really "huge" company than just a normal "large" company? The answer is actually "no." Big companies have large corporate staffs – financial, accounting, marketing, legal, engineering, strategic planning – to analyze and review virtually every proposal that comes to the CEO for a decision. Many people who have spent time working in corporations believe that running a smaller, more dynamic, growing company is probably harder than running a more mature corporation since the smaller company's CEO has less of a "deep bench" of talented support staff to help make day-to-day decisions.

This argument that "the bigger the company, the more the CEO should be paid" fails for another basic reason. There is nothing in economic theory to suggest large buyers should pay more than small buyers when they are buying the same thing. When ExxonMobil goes out and buys cars from Ford Motor they don't pay more per car than a smaller buyer. Nor do they pay more to buy a barrel of oil than a smaller oil company. In the labor market they don't pay any more for their secretaries, accountants, petroleum engineers or truck drivers than other companies a fraction of their size. So why would they pay more for their CEO?

When all else fails, defenders of inflated CEO pay point to baseball and football players. "Look how much they make," they say. "Aren't CEOs more important than ball players?" Of course, economists would answer that "importance" isn't relevant. If it were, schoolteachers would make more than CEOs, and they don't. What is relevant is how high the market price must be to induce people with the requisite talent to take the particular job.

When you look at the statistics, it appears that baseball players, for example, are actually underpaid compared to CEOs. The average major league baseball player's salary is about $5 million, considerably less than the average CEO. When you adjust for the relatively few players on each team that make true "CEO level" pay, the typical baseball player makes far less than the average, with over a third of them making about $500,000 or less. That's closer to what an upper middle-management executive might make in a corporation, but far below what the typical CEO is paid. When you consider that throwing or hitting a 90-plus mile-per-hour strike (something not taught in business schools) is a scarcer skill set than that possessed by most CEOs, it raises the question why ball players are actually not paid more than CEOs.

Finally, in Chapter 8, we talk about the consequences of paying thousands of CEOs way too much, compared to what their true economic cost would be if economics were actually allowed to operate. Is this a "victimless crime" where some people are getting undeservedly rich but it isn't really hurting anyone? Or is someone paying a price?

The answer is that our economy is paying a big price because "motivation matters." If you pay CEOs reasonable but not "over the top" salaries and bonuses, they take a longer-term, relationship-oriented approach to doing their job and building their business. If you pay them huge amounts, or give them compensation "lottery tickets" that can pay off in the tens and hundreds of millions of dollars if certain corporate events take place (big acquisitions, mergers, consolidations, etc.), then you are incentivizing CEOs to "swing for the fences" and try to do the big pay-off deals rather than build their businesses organically.

As we have seen in recent decades, big deals often pay off more for the CEOs and other top executives who do them, as well as for their Wall Street enablers who conceive, execute and finance the deals, than they do for the shareholders, workers, customers and other constituents of the companies that are affected.

In other words, creating incentives that are not economically valid for CEOs can lead to corporate actions that have no other economic purpose except to enrich the CEO and his/her cronies.

This finally brings us to the most important point of the book. The American people are not stupid. As voters recognize that corporate boards and CEOs take more of a "socialistic" approach to executive compensation than a free enterprise approach, with (1) all upside and no downside for CEOs and other top executives, and (2) a "suspension" of the law of supply and demand in the setting of CEO pay levels, they may decide they want similar benefits. That would threaten the political balance that has supported free enterprise policies for generations.

If people conclude that corporate executives and their boards of directors are essentially operating a "welfare state" for the CEO and top management class, then won't they demand similar protection from the risks of normal economic life for themselves? This is a serious political issue, and one that is just as critical to liberals as to conservatives, to Republicans as to Democrats. If we want voters to embrace free enterprise policies and a government that interferes as little as possible in the economic sphere, then we need to ensure that our free enterprise economy actually behaves like one, at every level.

Finally, how do we change this? Describing it correctly would be a good start. To deliberately and systematically pay CEOs substantially more than a free market would require is a misuse of corporate assets, just as much as sweetheart deals, embezzlement or other corrupt practices, and should be regarded as such. Boards of directors should be put on notice that approving such deals is a breach of their fiduciary duty to shareholders, and they should be called on it as necessary through shareholder suits, SEC actions and by the press.

INDEX

25247972R00095

Made in the USA
Middletown, DE
23 October 2015